THE RACE
TO THE
WHITE HOUSE

THE RACE TO THE WHITE HOUSE

CAMILLE PAGLIA

SHELBY STEELE

JAMES CARVILLE

DAVID GERGEN

Edited by Patrick Luciani and
Rudyard Griffiths

KEY PORTER BOOKS

Copyright © 2008 by Salon Speakers Limited

All rights reserved. No part of this work covered by the copyrights hereon may be reproduced or used in any form or by any means—graphic, electronic or mechanical, including photocopying, recording, taping or information storage and retrieval systems—without the prior written permission of the publisher, or, in case of photocopying or other reprographic copying, a licence from Access Copyright, the Canadian Copyright Licensing Agency, One Yonge Street, Suite 1900, Toronto, Ontario, M6B 3A9.

The race to the White House : the Grano speakers series, 2007-2008 / general editors, Patrick Luciani and Rudyard Griffiths.

ISBN 978-1-55470-109-4

1. Presidents--United States--Election--2008. 2. United States--Politics and government--2001- 3. Presidential candidates--United States. I. Luciani, Patrick II. Griffiths, Rudyard

JK526.2008R33 2008   324.973'0931   C2008-901606-8

The publisher gratefully acknowledges the support of the Canada Council for the Arts and the Ontario Arts Council for its publishing program. We acknowledge the support of the Government of Ontario through the Ontario Media Development Corporation's Ontario Book Initiative.

We acknowledge the financial support of the Government of Canada through the Book Publishing Industry Development Program (BPIDP) for our publishing activities.

Key Porter Books Limited
Six Adelaide Street East, Tenth Floor
Toronto, Ontario
Canada M5C 1H6

www.keyporter.com

Text design: Marijke Friesen
Electronic formatting: Alison Carr

Printed and bound in Canada

08 09 10 11 12 5 4 3 2 1

CONTENTS

Acknowledgments / 7
Preface / 9

ON HILLARY CLINTON Camille Paglia / 11
ON BARACK OBAMA Shelby Steele / 41
ON THE DEMOCRATIC LEADERSHIP RACE James Carville / 71
AN ELECTION FOR THE AGES David Gergen / 89

About the Contributors / 117
About the Editors / 119

ACKNOWLEDGMENTS

WHEN WE STARTED the Salon Speakers Series in 2004 at Toronto's Grano Restaurant, nothing would have happened without the generous support of our sponsors. Now we can thank them publicly for making the Grano Series the success it has become.

To start, we want to thank Allan Gotlieb and the Donner Canadian Foundation, Peter and Melanie Munk, and Joe and Sandra Rotman for having the foresight to see the importance of these events even before we did. They never interfered in our selection of speakers and encouraged us simply to bring in thinkers who would provoke and stimulate debate. They were there at the beginning and have remained loyal supporters throughout.

We also are extremely grateful to Richard Rooney at Burgundy Financial and Hugh MacKinnon at Bennett Jones for their encouragement and guidance, along with that of Hilary and Galen Weston. We have benefited immensely from their advice and sponsorship. We are also thankful to our other sponsors: Gerry Gluskin at Gluskin Sheff + Associates; the Delzotto brothers— Elvio, Angelo, and Leo at Tridel; Jim Doak at Megantic Investments; StrategyCorp; Spinelli Wines; Minto; Brian Crowley at The Atlantic Institute of Market Studies; and Roberto and Lucia Martella at Grano restaurant for allowing us to use their home for our series.

—Patrick Luciani and Rudyard Griffiths
Toronto 2008

PREFACE

WITH THESE FOUR TALKS on the U.S. election, Salon Speakers Ltd. continues the tradition of inviting exciting and important speakers to Toronto. In the intimate and informal atmosphere at Grano Restaurant, we have returned to the tradition of the intellectual "salon." This set of talks is the second group of lectures published since the series began in the fall of 2004. The first, entitled *American Power*, dealt with America's changing role in the world and the Middle East and was published in 2007.

The 2008 U.S. presidential campaign has turned out to be one of the most exciting in political memory. The race has been unique by virtue of its sheer unpredictability for both the Republican and Democratic parties. A year ago, Senator John McCain's campaign was in ruins with little chance of winning his party's nomination, and yet he managed to prevail not only against the talented Mitt Romney, former governor of Massachusetts, but also the conservative wing of his own party, who always doubted McCain's fiscal and social credentials.

But the real excitement is on the Democratic side. A race that was supposed to be over on Super Tuesday in February was really only the start. Senator Barack Obama, one of the most gifted and charismatic politicians ever to run for president, was in a fight to the end with the more experienced and tenacious Hillary Clinton, who was willing to take the battle to the Denver convention floor in August. As we write these words in early May, Obama has a clear edge in delegates and the popular vote—but anything can happen in this race to lead the Democrats in November.

Regardless of how things turn out, these four exciting talks, given in the fall of 2007 and early 2008, help us not only understand the candidates better, but give us some idea of what to expect in the general election of 2008.

—Patrick Luciani & Rudyard Griffiths
Toronto, May 2008

ON HILLARY CLINTON
Camille Paglia
September 18, 2007

THE FIRST TALK IN THE SERIES, by author and feminist Camille Paglia, gave an engaging overview of Hillary Clinton's candidacy. Ms. Paglia has been blunt in her assessment of Hillary, once writing a piece for *The New Republic* called "Ice Queen, Drag Queen." Ms. Paglia admires Mrs. Clinton for her tenacity and political intelligence, and says that no one has a better grasp of the issues. As well, Ms. Paglia points out that Hillary has the tough hide to withstand the "insane" criticism of being President of the United States. But she believes Hillary is too cynical for the post, with psychological flaws that will eventually undermine her. Her many scandals and the 1993 health policy failure follow her wherever she goes. Clinton's made-up story regarding her visit to Bosnia in the late 1990s only underlines her flaws. As one pundit put it, "The Clintons lie even when they don't have to." Ms.

Paglia says that when Hillary speaks, you get the rhetoric of the day; it changes depending on the polls. But more important, Hillary has no real connection with the common person. As for her husband Bill, Paglia asserts he's become a giant albatross around Clinton's neck.

Are Americans ready for a woman to be president? Absolutely, according to Paglia, but they aren't ready for Hillary. Paglia's choice would have been California senator Dianne Feinstein, a woman she greatly admires, and who she believes has the necessary gravitas to be president.

I HAVE BEEN ASKED to address the topic of Hillary Clinton and the 2008 presidential campaign. Let me start by saying that, as a longtime opponent of the Iraq war and as a registered Democrat, I am not at all confident that the Republicans will automatically be defeated next year. Anyone who thinks that the managerial ineptitude of the Bush White House, and the multiple disasters and embarrassments that have flowed from it, is going to rebound against the GOP is quite mistaken. The Republican party in the U.S. is running away from George Bush as fast as it can.

I faithfully listen to conservative talk radio, which is a very dynamic medium in the U.S. I listen to it all day long and into the night—when I'm not listening to sports radio, which is also of great sociological interest. Thus I can tell you that right now, because of the immigration crisis that has convulsed the Republican party, there is enormous animosity toward the Bush administration among rank and file Republicans. And, therefore, whoever is nominated by the Republicans is in no way going to run on George Bush's record. Bush is the past, and the error of the Democratic party lately is to think that George Bush is the target. This is absolute folly—to go on and on with this obsession with Bush, who is the biggest lame duck that anyone has seen in many a moon.

Forget it! The Democrats have to get themselves together on the question of geopolitics. The candidates need to project an authoritative persona and display some command of world history, some vision for the future. They need to provide some answer to the intractable problem of jihadism, which is not going to go away by anyone waving a wand. At the moment I feel we're heading toward a Republican victory. And I just don't understand the giddy, false confidence of my fellow Democrats.

Whoever the Democratic nominee, I will gladly vote for him or her. If it's Hillary Clinton, I will vote for her, but I'm hoping it's not! I just don't see how Hillary can win unless there is the kind of splintering of the Republican party that occurred in the election that brought Bill Clinton to the White House. Bill Clinton would not have been elected in 1992 had Ross Perot not led his renegade movement. George Bush the elder would have been a shoo-in were it not for Perot. If Hillary is the Democratic nominee, her only hope is that the nominee of the Republican Party isn't sufficiently conservative for the Republican rank and file, so that someone else is nominated, such as Newt Gingrich, as a protest third-party alternative. And it can happen.

My history of analyzing Hillary Clinton goes back a

long way—from the moment she arrived on the national scene in 1992. She and I are the same age, so there's a kind of parallel track. We were at Yale at the same time—I at the graduate school, she and her future husband at the law school across the street. We never knew each other, but we've had similar experiences, which is why I think I understand her and her aims and aspirations and limitations perhaps better than most.

I understand her in other ways, too. Her father was from Scranton, Pennsylvania, where some of my relatives live. I was born not far away in the Southern Tier of upstate New York in a factory town—Endicott—so I understand the working-class roots of that area and the kind of hardscrabble life her father's family had led. Even though Hillary grew up in the affluent Chicago suburbs, her voice sometimes curiously reverts to the harsh Scranton accent—it's something she deliberately uses when speaking to working-class voters.

Hillary's family became prosperously middle class, but her father earned an income by essentially doing manual labor from their home. He ran a one-man drapery business. And the way her home was run in childhood, successive biographies have revealed, was almost as a kind of prison. I think it's pretty clear that her father was psychologically abusive toward her mother and brothers and that the sunny picture Hillary painted of her childhood in her memoir and elsewhere is a falsehood.

You can see it in the strained smile in her early pictures. She's like little Miss Perfect, smiling brightly while her brothers look moody or miserable—those two ne'er-do-well brothers, who have been such failures as adults. Hillary's brothers will always be a huge embarrassment to her campaign; they've repeatedly dragged her down, and she's had to bail them out of trouble.

But Hillary is enormously competitive. She formed her personality in that strange, high-pressure household where her father was irrational, demanding and peremptory. Thus her vision of men is distorted. Hillary's attitude, evidently learned from her mother, is that women must endure and save men from their worst selves. Men are basically flawed—they're children. It's women who are the strength of human history. Whatever men do, women must tolerate it. You go to church and receive God's blessing and then return to your mission to save society from man's depredations.

There's a kind of twisted psychology in all this that helped produce the Clintons' notoriously dysfunctional marriage, where Bill misbehaves and Hillary helps cover it up. I have never understood the silence of my fellow feminists on this matter. Bill Clinton projects an image of geniality, kindness, generosity—I understand that he's extremely popular in Canada! But what has been overlooked in his history is his abusiveness toward women—in particular working-class and lower-middle-class women—which normally would send feminists into a tailspin. It's been tolerated, however, because of the general liberalism of his policies.

One of the main things I, as a feminist, hold against Hillary is the way she has systematically enabled Bill Clinton's womanizing by trashing his accusers' characters. As a product of Wellesley College—one of the glossy, elite Seven Sisters colleges—and of Yale Law School, Hillary has the attitude that she belongs to the superior class of woman, the truly valuable woman. Lower-middle-class women, on the other hand—such as staffers at the White House or the Arkansas governor's mansion or State House—or working-class women, such as Paula Jones, are trash. If these women say or do anything to endanger the Clintons' career, they must be destroyed.

You hear this attitude very clearly from the proxies the Clintons regularly use—such as James Carville, who was the "war room" mastermind of the first Clinton victory in 1992. Carville has a football mentality. He's an amusing man whom I personally like, but he is absolutely ruthless. He has exported his Machiavellian brand of campaign politics around the world and it's made him millions of dollars as a campaign consultant.

Carville is the one who said of Paula Jones' accusations, "Drag a hundred dollar bill through a trailer park, and there's no telling what you'll find." That was the way he dealt with Paula Jones' justified complaint about the way she had been solicited and callously treated by Bill Clinton. It was a case of overt sexual harassment of a state employee that my fellow feminists have been absolutely silent on.

Never mind all these flaws, however! In the U.S. we desperately need a woman in the White House. I hope to see a woman president during my lifetime. I can't think of anything more important from a feminist point of view. We are lagging enormously behind the rest of the world here. But it is not true that Hillary Clinton is the first serious woman candidate for the presidency. There is a long line of female candidates going back to the nineteenth century, including Victoria Woodhull, who was a radical feminist at odds with her fellow feminists. A series of prominent women have put themselves forward for the presidency, such as Bella Abzug, Patricia Schroeder and Shirley Chisholm, who was African American. Perhaps the most credible candidate thus far was a Republican, Elizabeth Dole, who simply could not get the financing to continue.

Here's the problem: we have an insane system of campaigning in the U.S. that is dependent on raising money. Money for what? For millions of bloody dollars for buying TV ads and consultants who have made a fortune off of advising our candidates. Well, who the hell cares about TV anymore? Everyone has moved to the Web. As a consequence of this endless fundraising grind, many excellent candidates don't put themselves forward.

My favorite woman candidate would be Senator Dianne

Feinstein of California, who was once the mayor of San Francisco. I think she should have been the first woman president. This is a woman of tremendous deliberative gravitas, with deep knowledge of the military through her service on Senate military committees. She first came to national attention in 1978 because of her amazing coolness under fire when the mayor of San Francisco and a gay city councilman were assassinated in their offices by a deranged fellow councilman. Dianne Feinstein, as the president of the board of supervisors who would now automatically become the mayor, had to go before the media at that traumatic moment and announce that these murders had occurred right there in City Hall.

I will never forget seeing that on TV. I said, "Who *is* that woman?" She was amazing: you could see her deep emotion and yet also her disciplined, authoritative control. I had never seen such sense of command by a woman politician in an emergency. I said, "That woman should be president," and I began to follow her career with interest. I've always been very impressed with her when she is interviewed on TV talk shows. She is centered, she has core values, and she does not veer all over the place, according to what consultants are telling her.

But when Hillary speaks on camera, what you get is the rhetoric of the day. The spin changes from day to day depending on the polls. Hillary is smart, but everything she says is by rote. Yes, she can talk at great length; yes, she can give strong speeches; but everything is highly conceptualized and planned. Hillary has no emotional intelligence, no real intuition or instinct for the stage. She feigns connection with the common person, but that's not the company she keeps. Nevertheless, she is a woman of great experience in politics, a woman who knows the Washington bureaucracy and who won't act like a newbie when she arrives in Washington.

Hillary has a tough hide. That's extremely important in this day of the modern media. For anyone, male or female, to survive in politics in the U.S., you have to be ready to take a hail of criticism of the most insane kind. In fact, the campaign trail is a rite of passage where candidates are besieged with a rain of insults and false accusations as well as the resurrection of every dark skeleton from years long past. I think it's important for any leader to be able to maintain focus. It's almost an anthropological principle of history. As a leader, you may be elevated to the top through some wave of popularity, but the moment you reach the top, there's some eternal human impulse that kicks into action to tear you down. You have to be prepared for that. Hillary Clinton is hard-bitten and cynical from experience, and I don't think that should be discounted in this era when any emergency can strike. You can't be knocked off stride simply by some rude article in the newspaper.

At any rate, the Clintons emerged pretty suddenly from obscurity. Bill Clinton had made a much-commented-on speech to the 1988 Democratic convention that went on too long—when he said, "in conclusion," people applauded! But Clinton, a centrist Southern governor, was nevertheless seen as the wave of the future. Clinton only got into the presidential race when Mario Cuomo withdrew. Cuomo, then governor of New York, would have probably made a fine president, but he thought the reelection of the elder George Bush was inevitable; so he didn't run. That was a terrible mistake, because Cuomo would have had a clear shot at the White House.

So Bill Clinton arrived on the national scene essentially unvetted. The national media, so eager for a Democratic candidate, failed to do a thorough inquiry into his past. And there were plenty of scandals involving women—women, women everywhere in his past in Little Rock. All of this burst upon us with the Gennifer Flowers case, while Clinton was still on the road in his 1992 campaign. Flowers was a voluptuous Southern blonde, whom I had the pleasure to hear sing at her nightclub off Bourbon Street in New Orleans a couple of years ago—the year before Hurricane Katrina hit and put her club out of business. I can assure you that, even now, Gennifer Flowers exudes a sexual charisma that demonstrates why Bill Clinton would have been smitten with her for twelve years. I believe every one of her allegations about her affair with Bill!

So the Clintons burst on the national scene, and the liberal mainstream media didn't ask enough questions about Bill Clinton's past. But for many members of my generation of 1960s women, Hillary was very refreshing. I was a fan of Hillary from the start. I thought she was great! For example, during the 1992 campaign, I was on *The Phil Donahue Show* with Susan Faludi, my opponent in feminism. Near the end of the debate, Donahue said, "I have something to show you," and he ran the news footage from that very day where Hillary had been asked something on the road, and she snapped, "Well, I could have stayed home and baked cookies and had teas." That line is going to stick to her forever because it seemed like she was dissing homemakers from her position as a pricey, Ivy League–bedecked lawyer. But I thought it was hilarious and wonderful—that sharp sardonic woman's voice. I thought, "Yeah, that's the voice of my generation!" Susan Faludi and I turned to each other after we had been warring for the whole program, and we enthusiastically said, "Yes, we like Hillary Clinton." It was the *only* thing we agreed on—and we've agreed on nothing else ever since!

On Inauguration Day there was also a moment that I was very fond of but that's been totally forgotten now. At the public reception, people who had lined up outside were filing into the White House as part of the celebration, but there was some sort of snafu. Suddenly, Hillary, not realizing there was an open mike, said to Bill, "Listen, there are people out there getting screwed!" I thought, "Wow, there it is again—the voice of my generation of women" who wanted to use four-letter words like sailors, who wanted to break through bourgeois decorum, who wanted to remake the image of the professional woman. So I was a Hillary fan.

But then, on that same day, I had a little qualm as I watched the Clintons on TV at the Inauguration gala. As Barbra Streisand was singing, I thought it was very odd that Hillary Clinton, in her designer gown, was sitting there scowling with a glowering look that seemed totally inappropriate for that festive occasion. I mentioned it a year later in a debate on CNN's now-expired show, *Crossfire*, with Ann Lewis—who continues to be a hired flunky for Hillary Clinton. Lewis said, "Oh, please—you're talking about an expression on someone's face, with all these policy decisions that are so much more important?"

Well, Ann Lewis probably knew bloody well then what the rest of us didn't know for years—that Bill Clinton may have had a dalliance with Ms. Streisand and that Hillary was in a big snit about it that day, which was why she was glowering as Streisand sang. My attitude remains that no matter what was bothering her, Hillary had an obligation on that important occasion to show a persona of graciousness. The problems in the Clinton marriage that were revealed on Inauguration Day were a premonition of what was going to come during the Lewinsky scandal, which brought the government to a standstill.

Newspapers began calling me early on to comment on Hillary. My first big piece on Hillary was a 1993 cover story of the *Sunday Times* magazine in London. The headline—not written by me!—was "Kind of a Bitch: Why I Like Hillary Clinton." However, I, along with many of my fellow Democrats, became very disillusioned with her that year because of the way she fumbled the health-care–reform initiative. This was a very important moment in American politics: we desperately needed health-care reform, and the issue had tremendous momentum. Republicans too believed that reform was urgent and were looking for solutions. But Hillary handled it in the most ham-handed way. She would not even reveal the names of the hundreds of panel members and advisers who were working through all these labyrinthine, bureaucratic, futuristic, Big Brother proposals that she had put forward. It was an absolute fiasco.

This was the first year of the Clinton presidency. Why would Bill Clinton put his wife in charge of that massive reform attempt, when one-sixth of the national budget was tied up in medical care? And why would he foolishly promise, "We're going to have this report to you in a hundred days"? What an artificial and unrealistic deadline. Bill was waving a plastic card around for the cameras and saying, "This is all you'll need, this one card!" Well, of course, everyone thought, "Oh, good Lord, we're going to have a master computer with everyone's private health-care information on it."

There were a million legitimate questions that people had that were never answered, and the whole scheme fell of its own weight. So Americans have been waiting fifteen long years for health-care reform to be put back on the table. Now all the leading Democratic nominees for the presidential nomination have their own individual health-care proposals. They don't really differ that much, except that Hillary's is mandatory, with penalties included. So I think it would be an issue very vulnerable to attack from Republicans next year.

Then there was the endless series of scandals throughout the nineties as one thing after another came up from Hillary's past—the Whitewater controversy and so on. I ended up writing a very notorious cover story for *The New Republic* in 1996 called "Ice Queen, Drag Queen," where I said that Hillary's whole persona as a woman is essentially a drag queen impersonation. I stand by every word I wrote, although it took the rest of the media years to catch up to it. I continue to believe that it's Hillary's psychological flaws and ambiguities, and not just her policy positions, that will undermine her candidacy next year. I just can't see people crossing party lines in the numbers needed to vote for her.

It's not because Hillary's a woman; that charge of sexism is absurd. I think the U.S. is ready to elect a woman president. There are, for example, many prominent, outspoken women conservatives right now, including female pundits, columnists, talk show hosts and so on. I think the time is right for a woman leader. But it's just that this particular woman may not be the right woman. She has so much baggage that the Republicans are shrewdly holding back on. It's quite obvious that they want Hillary to be the nominee: she would be the easiest by far to defeat.

Part of the problem is Hillary's relationship to social class, which I think is very troublesome. She was embarrassed in some way by her father and her relatives, and she has run away from it in ways I find dismaying. I am very uncomfortable with how Hillary bonds with people of wealth and power and, in particular, the frivolous Hollywood elite. I'm a lifelong fan of popular culture, but I have disdain for most of the current Hollywood elite. I think they're mostly airheads and that the quality of product coming from the American entertainment industry these days is extremely poor. The way the Clintons' heads are so easily turned by showbiz personalities is highly embarrassing. But it's symptomatic of trends in American politics over the past twenty years. For example, I think that former Senator Fred Thompson, a Republican candidate for president, made a terrible mistake in announcing his candidacy on a late-night talk show. I mean, what have we been reduced to when talk shows become the stage for an announcement of such gravity for the most powerful position in the world? It's tacky!

There was a notorious cover of the *National Enquirer* tabloid showing the Clintons' Hollywood pals jumping up and down as if on a trampoline on the bed in the historic

Lincoln Bedroom in the White House. They were going, "Yay! We're here now!" What absolute juvenility that the Lincoln Bedroom was turned over to an endless series of Hollywood parakeets, whom the Clintons met through their friendship with Linda Bloodworth-Thomason, the producer and creator of *Designing Women*, and whom they knew from Arkansas. It was Bloodworth-Thomason who was probably behind Hillary's makeover for her Senate campaign—the pantsuits and chic hairstyles and so on. At the present moment, Hillary is basically a Hollywood product.

Nevertheless, we have to ask whether the imperative to have a woman in the highest office is so urgent a matter for the United States that we can overlook all of Hillary's faults. What kind of president would she make? Well, number one, she's highly organized; she's a workaholic who doesn't see recreation as part of human life. She appears not to enjoy life in any natural way. She has become a kind of artificial personality. I feel that she's haunted by the past and is therefore obsessively focused on the future. But such people can be very useful and productive in public office.

My main problem with Hillary is that, while she might be very organized, I honestly don't see her talent as an executive or leader. She would be better suited as a cabinet officer or as an ambassador to the UN. I mean, would she really be able to manage the government bureaucracy, to give it a sense of morale or spirit? She is too stridently partisan. She has a kind of Manichean mentality; everything is black or white. There are, in her view, all these evil people in the world who oppose the Clintons—who aim only for the betterment of humanity, who have no self-interest whatever, and who have been defamed by a vast right-wing conspiracy as well as by enemies within the party.

Hillary is a thoroughgoing Methodist, a very determined and sometimes grim social activist. She has a tremendous power of denial. She evidently thinks that she is the beneficiary of God's grace. It's a nearly Puritan bequest: God has a mission for her, and therefore anything that she does is positive, and anyone who opposes her must be destroyed. This attitude is not the most positive ideal for politics, which demands consensus, a give-and-take. You can't always achieve your aim. So Hillary's programmatic rigidity sometimes turns into a delusional projection for a utopian future, which she believes is going to come to pass through big government.

There's been a lot of reporting over the years that most of the disasters of the Clinton regime can be traced back to Hillary: the strategic misjudgments from the firing of the entire travel office of career employees, who were dear to the media, to the refusal to settle with Paula Jones, which led directly to the Lewinsky imbroglio. (Monica's name emerged during the discovery process in Jones' lawsuit.) The Monica Lewinsky scandal paralyzed the American government for two years and anyone who doesn't see that is blind: the government was tied up by Bill Clinton protecting himself.

That man should have resigned that first month; he was close to doing it but decided to fight it out. The senior members of his party had almost convinced him to resign. He should have resigned out of shame for what he had done. Al Gore would have been president while his reputation was still high. Gore would have gotten his sea legs in office and, I believe, would have been reelected. By the time he did run, he had become a fool, the prisoner of Naomi Wolf and his daughter Karenna, Ivy League airheads with a bizarre gender-based dream vision of what Al Gore should be. So instead of the real Al Gore—conservative, steady and boring in a three-piece blue pin-striped suit, looking like a diplomat and an authority figure—we had him bouncing around the country showing off his buff chest and wearing earth tones.

It was a tragedy, what happened to Al Gore. I didn't vote for him in 2000, but I wish I had been able to. I voted for Ralph Nader instead and I don't regret it. So go ahead and blame me for the election of Bush! But in all candor, I don't feel that Al Gore would have been the strongest president to face the challenge of 9/11. The threat of world terrorism had been marginalized by the Clinton-Gore administration and completely ignored while the Lewinsky scandal was consuming the government. The Clinton administration was appallingly nonresponsive to the first attack on the World Trade Center in 1993. In the late nineties, I was warning about that in Salon.com. Why was the U.S. so passive and oblivious? It seemed obvious that there was a growing terrorist problem out there.

But who was our National Security Advisor? Sandy Berger, a genial guy who maybe should have been a dog catcher. Berger had no credentials whatsoever to be National Security Advisor to the president. And Berger should be in prison right now. He stole documents from the National Archives about the Clinton administration's handling of security issues—stuffing documents into his socks and hiding them under a trailer outside the building. And Bill Clinton goes on TV and laughs it off: "Oh, that's Sandy. Everyone knew how messy his desk was!" This was *his* National Security Advisor as jihadism was rising around the world? Canada, get over your infatuation with Bill Clinton! You're living in an illusion—9/11 was the terrible result of Clinton's problems and failures.

Anyway, back to Hillary. Hillary has had great trouble finding an authentic personal voice. Recently she went into an African American church and carried on: "This is the day the Lord has made!" Good heavens, it was pure Aunt Jemima! Obama, on the other hand, has a perfect right to use African American locutions and Southern intonations. He was a community organizer in African American neighborhoods in Chicago. But Hillary has never had that kind of experience—she's just a tourist. Her condescending assumption that African American women are going to support her because of her husband is utterly insulting to the capabilities of the African American electorate—which is why Oprah Winfrey's embrace of Barack Obama came as such a blow. Hillary had assumed that she had Oprah, and all the rest of the major media, in her pocket.

Hillary's voice problem was obvious recently when she was questioning General David Petraeus as he was making his report about the putative success of the surge in Iraq. Hillary had clearly been coached to talk softly, so as not to offend TV viewers with her usual stridency. But her voice ended up as an annoyingly monotonous undertone. Why does every single thing she does seem feigned? Why is there this sense that she's never entirely natural, that she never just speaks from her heart? We feel *the plan* too clearly. That air of falseness, her discomfort in public, is going to undermine her in the long run. The leading Republican candidates have all been far more natural—they seem like real guys. Whether it was Mitt Romney or Rudy Giuliani or Fred Thompson, when they were being interviewed on talk shows or on the road, people shoved microphones in their faces, and these candidates showed a sense of spontaneity and fun. It's because they, unlike Hillary, have consistent core values.

The latest item trotted out by the Hillary campaign is that she is the new Margaret Thatcher. She is like the Iron Lady. She has strength—and you notice how Hillary is always saying the word "strength" over and over? She has the "strength" to lead the nation. Well, excuse me. Margaret

Thatcher, whatever you might think of her, had strong core values. She had one ideology and was persistent and consistent in pushing it forward. You never were in any doubt as to where Thatcher stood. She did not rely on consultants to spoon-feed her talking points, and she did not think every morning, "Oh, what shall I say today?" She spoke from her own unique position at all times. There is absolutely no basis of comparison between Margaret Thatcher and Hillary Clinton.

A better comparison would be to Dianne Feinstein who, in my view, never strikes a false note. When Senator Feinstein speaks, she's able to combine a sense of compassion and feeling with intellect and knowledge. It's a wonderful fusion—a quality that should be possessed by our first woman president. But nevertheless, if it turns out that Hillary proves to be the strongest candidate of a flawed lot and we end up with her in the White House, it will be a great experiment. If she fails, it's still important that Hillary be respected as a pioneer in terms of her ability to put together this massive money-making campaign. Relying on her husband's contacts and knowledge, she has been able to set up a national organization for extorting money—which has now led her into more scandals, such as the Norman Hsu case. It's a bit embarrassing. But Hillary has laid the groundwork for the first successful woman president. Women candidates of either party will follow the map she has made.

A main issue right now is the giant albatross around her neck, Bill Clinton. For a while it seemed that Hillary was running on her own and that Bill Clinton, who loves to hog the spotlight, was remaining decorously in the background. But as her campaign started to flounder, he moved much more aggressively into the foreground in ways that make me uneasy as a feminist. I mean, surely we don't want the first woman president coming into office on the coattails of her husband?

When Bill's around and they're campaigning as a team, as they did in New Hampshire, she is more relaxed because he has an intuitive feeling for the crowd: he's a great performer. He loves touchy-feely contact with people, whereas she is stiffer and much more standoffish. I think her consultants feel that when they're together, it projects a more natural feeling about her, but let's face it—at this point, it's a pretend marriage between two people who hardly see each other.

Q: I don't get it, why are you a Democrat?
A: Well, I believe in the necessity for social justice. I believe that the government does have an obligation to provide basic medical care and decent housing to the poor. I do believe the government must play a major role for people who cannot provide for themselves. This is where I diverge

from the Republican party, which doesn't support any of those things. However, I am not a big government Democrat. I am highly suspicious of any centralized bureaucracy, which eventually becomes a parasitic labyrinth. I'm a libertarian Democrat: I believe that there should be limited government intrusion into our private lives.

Republicans on the whole, although there are some exceptions, don't feel that the government owes anyone anything. The government is there simply as a basic service; taxes should be reduced to the absolute minimum; and health care is not a right. I agree that it's not a right. I simply feel that health care is owed to needy people in an affluent society. One cannot tolerate such a grotesque disparity and inequity between the very rich and the very poor.

That's why I support the Democratic party. But I have to say that it's the Democratic party of the Hubert Humphrey period that I feel closest to. There was once a more populist Democratic party with a much stronger working-class base. The present lawyer-laden meritocracy that Hillary Clinton represents is a kind of elitist departure from and rejection of the party's original working-class roots. Forty years ago, working-class people started to migrate to the Republican side, which continues to be far more sympathetic to the small businessman.

Q: Bill and Hillary Clinton have been selected by your party for fourteen years to represent them. I can't quite see how somebody as open-minded, intelligent and knowledgeable as you could not join the Republican Party.

A: I respect the Republicans because many of my relatives were, in fact, Nixon Democrats. My family members were originally shoe-factory workers who emigrated to the U.S. from Italy. They belonged to the Franklin Delano Roosevelt generation and were lifelong Democrats until all of the chaos of the sixties, caused by my generation. They drifted to the Republican side because of the disorder in the streets: they voted for Richard Nixon and still usually vote Republican.

So I think I understand and certainly respect the Republican position. I simply feel that the role of government should be more actively compassionate than many contemporary conservatives believe, especially on the issues of health care, housing and education. I think that the state of urban education for African Americans in the inner cities is a disaster and that there's an appalling neglect of the physical condition of poor neighborhoods. It's scandalous. I just feel that my party has more of a chance because of its basic principles of remediation—even though little is ever done from one Democratic administration to the next, despite all the promises.

Q: Speaking of earth tones and the earth and global warming and Al Gore, do you believe that he will throw his hat in the ring, and if not, why not?

A: It would be interesting if he did; it would certainly disorder the entire race. I am very skeptical of Al Gore. I think he's a kind of fantasist. I feel sorry for him. He suffered for a long time in the shadow of his very accomplished and politically powerful father. I think Gore is much too vulnerable to the women around him. It's as if he lacks a clear sense of masculine identity.

And he was raised in a bubble of privilege, despite that Tennessee country accent, which he's always pulling stagily out in public. Believe me, at home he speaks perfectly standard English! Gore grew up in a posh hotel in Washington and then went through prep schools and Harvard—where he flunked science, by the way! I see him as this mournful character who lives in a dream world.

People have indeed been speculating that if Gore suddenly appeared in this election like a jack-in-the-box, it would totally throw the race open and many Democrats who are worried about Hillary would rush to him. But campaigning is a very hard job, and I think it brutalized him the first time. That's the problem with American politics: national campaigning shouldn't be so life and spirit killing. It drives some of our best potential candidates out of the race. Why should anyone subject themselves to this horrible process? So what we get are these monsters of ambition, twisted deformed characters like Hillary Clinton, who at this point has become a kind of late Bette Davis character.

Q: I wanted to ask you a question about Oprah Winfrey. I wanted to ask you about your thoughts on her as a political influence, as a cultural force. What influence has she had on feminism in the United States, or perhaps farther than that, and what about her political ambitions, either directly or indirectly, particularly now, given the support she has given Barack Obama?

A: I faithfully watched the Oprah show from the moment it went national in the eighties. I've ceased watching it now because Oprah has become such a mega-celebrity in her own right and no longer has the common touch that she did in the very beginning. I liked the heavy Oprah— the Oprah who would just sit there and take the hand of her guest and cry along with her. The show ran in real time; that is, it went on continuously for the full hour, so you would be able to follow all the traumas step by step, as the guests revealed the abuses of their past. Oprah would feel deeply, and you would feel deeply. It was just one grand emotional fest!

Now, because of her mammoth success, the show is basically an industrial product. There's Oprah presiding from on high and barely being able to tolerate any of it. You can see her boredom with the whole thing. The show is now way overproduced. Oprah's up on stage, while the guests are in a huge audience far below; she's like a Roman emperor looking down at the gladiators. "What do you think, Marisa Berenson? Oh, okay, fine." On to the next person—boom, boom, boom. It's become so rude. And now the show is taped over ninety minutes or two hours or more, and then it's quickly cut down to less than an hour in this ham-handed way by people in the editing booth in Chicago. Jump, jump, jump—so there's no emotional continuity any longer. It's such a loss.

But Oprah changed the world. There are now shows all over the world in every language where you see a glamorously dressed host sitting there holding the hand of so-and-so from a peasant village as she relates the saga of her abusive husband. The talk show host has become a kind of popular messiah, with the blessing and the laying on of hands and the healing. It's definitely become a kind of quasi-religious ritual.

Oprah is obviously a phenomenon. She has launched a successful magazine with herself on the front cover every single month. She's become a kind of divinity in her own right. The whole publishing industry in America knows that the moment Oprah chooses a book, it becomes an instant bestseller, moving millions of copies out of the stores. She's done a great public service by encouraging reading. But she's a strange character. At her houses, you never see a TV. All her TVs are shut up in furniture boxes—did you know that? She says she doesn't ever want to see a TV at home. On her recent cross-country trip with her friend Gayle King, she wouldn't let Gayle play the radio because Oprah had to be alone with her thoughts!

So Oprah is *deep*, okay? Oprah is deep in her way. We'll see whether she can transfer the success that she can endow on books to a presidential candidate like Barack Obama. I'm hoping she can!

Q: Immigration policy: discuss.
A: It's inevitable that if you have so much poverty and overpopulation in Mexico and a much more affluent country across the border, you're going to get a natural mass migration, as has happened at every point in history. But especially now, post 9/11, with our elevated security concerns, we can see the failure, ineptitude and incompetence of the Bush administration in dealing with these border issues in a rational way.

I mean, for heaven's sakes, Canada certainly seems to have far stricter borders. How many times have I been stopped at immigration? It happened again today! They asked me, "What are you here for?" I said, "To give a talk." "On what?" "On American politics." I was flagged immediately! I was sent to immigration—the only such person on my flight—and I was interrogated before I was let go. This also happened in 1992, when I was foolishly naive about Canadian rules. The customs agent asked, "What are you here for?" I said, "To give a lecture." And he asked, "On what?" I said, "Sex." Flagged! They sent me off to immigration immediately—once again, the only such person on my flight. On my visit last year, however, I got by.

The agent asked, "What are you here for?" And I said, "Oh, I'm on a book tour." "On what subject?" "Poetry." I sailed right through! Poetry is perfectly fine with Canadian customs.

So it seems that Canada is far more organized and regulated on border issues. But the immigration issue is absolutely convulsing politics in the U.S. I think it's going to loom very large in the national election next year, and the nominees will be heavily scrutinized for their positions on it. This presents a difficult problem for the Democrats, because the party's core constituencies are militant ethnic minorities. So there's not much room to maneuver there.

I hear call-ins on radio talk shows complaining about the constant crime problems from immigrants in suburban Los Angeles, Arizona, Texas, or Oklahoma and even in communities in the upper Midwest and South. People will call up and angrily say, "We can't leave our child's bicycle or tricycle on the lawn—everything is immediately stolen. We have these undocumented people coming in from Mexico, and it has got to be stopped!" I suspect it's going to produce a wave of xenophobia and ultimately a racist backlash if the government doesn't get control of immigration policy. Right now, I have no answers for it. It's an absolutely inflammatory and explosive issue that the Democrats are running away from.

ON BARACK OBAMA
Shelby Steele
October 25, 2007

SHELBY STEELE, AUTHOR and senior fellow at Stanford University, has written extensively about race in America. He has been severely critical of black leaders holding back black America through misguided social policies.

According to Steele in this lecture, white guilt has led directly to the debilitating roles of affirmative action and welfare, which have helped destroy the traditional black family. A steady welfare check has replaced the role of fathers in black families, and affirmative action has brought into question the legitimate accomplishments of talented blacks in American society.

Steele discusses two masks in black American history: the challenger and the bargainer. The first, exemplified by Jesse Jackson and Al Sharpton, holds the premise that whites are racists and must work to prove otherwise. The bargainer, on the other hand, avoids making whites feel guilty as long as they can practice their craft. Classic bargainers are Tiger Woods, Oprah Winfrey and Louis Armstrong.

It is this world of masks that Barack Obama enters, trying to be an iconic bargainer in the rough world of politics. In his book on Obama entitled *The Bound Man*, Steele makes the argument that Obama is a divided man who can't be black enough for African Americans, but is too black for white America. And because of that, Steele doesn't see Obama winning the White House.

I KNOW YOUR SERIES is on politics and so that's what I want to talk about, primarily focusing on Barack Obama. But I'd like to put him in a little context first, and talk about white guilt and then move more directly to Obama himself.

I think one of the truly great and unacknowledged forces at work in American society today is white guilt. White guilt, I think, comes from this great postwar series of revolutions around the world, not just in America but in India with Ghandi, across Africa and across Asia where Europe was pushed back into its boundaries. In the United States, there was the civil rights movement.

Though many of these wars flew under the flag of communism or nationalism, they were basically wars against the principle of white supremacy—the idea that being white constituted a moral authority in and of itself. If a white man and a black man met on a path in Africa, the black man was expected to carry the white man's baggage.

That was the idea that prevailed for centuries, and so I think most of the revolutions after World War II were against that single idea: the idea of white supremacy. They were in argument with the idea that white supremacy constituted an authority, that it gave whites an entitlement. And so all those revolutions were out to defeat that larger idea of authority. They all succeeded. Every single one of those revolutions prevailed. There's no record of any defeat. White supremacy was defeated *as an authority* around the world.

In the United States, at the height of the civil rights victories in the sixties, the idea that whites were superior no longer carried any weight. This was a marvelous human achievement that has pretty much gone unremarked in the world. The other side, of course, is that once you acknowledge that white supremacy is wrong, that it is an illegitimate source of authority, and you say, "Oh, we're sorry. We were wrong," then you become stigmatized with that idea. So now, having admitted that racism was practiced, the stigma of being racist falls on whites.

Now any black in America could walk up and say, "You're a racist." There's really no convincing way to say, "Well, no I'm not. I really am not." This circumstance of presumed guilt is white guilt. Living with the presumption of guilt forces whites to act guiltily even if they feel no guilt.

That became an enormous power for black Americans that we still, of course, wield and rely on today, sad to say, and it has changed the very nature of our society: whites are now stigmatized as racist and are in the position of forever having to prove a negative that, "I'm not racist," which of course is impossible to do. We blacks delight in that impossibility and exploit it to its maximum. This is the state of affairs.

Whites have been in this position, I believe, since the mid-sixties when, in order to establish their decency as individuals, their legitimacy as institutions, they had to find a way to conspicuously dissociate themselves from this racist stigma. "No, not me. I'm not racist."

I think much of our domestic policy dealing with race in the United States—all of it, really—is what I call "dissociational" policy. It has no real purpose other than to dissociate institutions from the stigma of being seen as racist.

The Great Society was the first dissociational program. "We're going to end poverty in our time. And we're going to throw billions of dollars at it," and so forth. Well, was the goal at that point really to end poverty or was it to dissociate the American government and society from its history of racism?

Affirmative action is another example. The welfare policies that came out of the late sixties and early seventies whereby the government simply gave out a little-better-than-a-subsistence living primarily to blacks, and then asked absolutely nothing whatsoever of them: "Here's money. The only rule you have to follow is that you can't be married." A wonderful incentive to form a stable family life.

Well, how thoughtless. What a **mindlessly cruel** social

policy. Of course, it had a more negative impact on the black family than segregation did. Even slavery was not able to defeat the black family in the way these welfare policies did—Uncle Sam saying, "The man that is in your life is iffy. I'm here every month, first of the month. I'll be there for you. So what would you want him for?" As I like to say, if you instituted that same policy in Pebble Beach, California, you'd probably break the family there as well.

The human blindness of these policies makes the point that their purpose was to dissociate the society, the government and its institutions from the stigma of racism rather than actually help the people who were poor and in need.

Universities must have diversity programs, must have affirmative action programs. They don't care one bit whether they help blacks or not. If you're black, you're going to get affirmative action whether you want it or you don't. It's going to be imposed on you. "If it stigmatizes you, too bad. If it ruins your reputation for excellence, too bad. Its purpose is not you. It's about us. We need to be seen as a legitimate institution and, in order to do that, we have to practice these kinds of dissociational policies."

This is the landscape that someone like Barack Obama enters when he enters American politics. He enters a society that is wracked, not with a genuine guilt of conscience, "Oh, I'm anguished over what happened to blacks"—that's not how white guilt works—but a stigma of racism, a society that must fight and struggle in everything it does, in all of its endeavors, to prove that it is not racist.

I've written some pieces on war, and white guilt is even a factor in the way we now fight wars. When we go to war as a society, we're now in the position of having to fight for our legitimacy, our right to go to war, our right to fight, more than we fight to win the war.

What's important is that we establish America's legitimacy; that we're not this old, racist, imperialist Western society beating up on this Third World nation of brown people who are weak. If it takes losing the war in order to make this point, then maybe it's better to lose—better to lose than be judged racist.

White guilt is, I believe, an extraordinarily powerful force and exerts itself in every level of society. I'm going to come back to this in a minute.

So Barack Obama comes on the political scene. Let me talk about him just as a man for a moment, as an individual. The one thing I think that's obvious to most people is that Obama is enormously talented as a politician. Few people have come on the political scene with those kinds of skills, with that ability to articulate complex issues easily, fluidly. There's no other candidate on either side of the aisle who has that ability.

He has written two books. His second book, I think, is just sort of the usual political book but the first book is a marvelous, beautifully written, honest, courageous memoir in which he looks at the most difficult aspects of his life, the deepest conflicts, the beginnings of his family, his abandonment by a father at the age of two, his circumstances of being raised by a white mother and grandparents in Hawaii and so forth. And he looks at all this with the courage that you would expect a really good writer to have. He finds his strength in his honesty. It's a marvelous book and I recommend it to you.

Again, I'm impressed by somebody with that kind of facility, that kind of talent, entering American politics. Certainly his talents are part of what have made him an exciting and charismatic figure in many ways.

Another aspect of Barack Obama that is important is the fact that—like all American blacks—he is at risk of being stigmatized by affirmative action. For example, suppose you see in the paper tomorrow morning that somebody has been appointed superintendent of schools in some city and the face in the picture is black. Instantly, reflexively you say, "Well, of course. Affirmative action. He got the job in part because he's black."

And so then we say, "Well, all right. You know, we have to live with that. That's the way things are." I think that would have been the case for Barack Obama. There was no way for him to avoid the affirmative action stigma. It is an imposed policy. Everybody gets it, even those blacks who don't remotely need it. Bill Cosby's kids get affirmative action and carry the stigma of affirmative action.

So he got it as well. There was nothing he could do

about it. But then he did something remarkable. He became the editor of the *Harvard Law Review*. The only way you can get that position is through merit. This was the birth of the Barack Obama that we know. This achievement separated him from the stigma of inferiority that goes with affirmative action. The *Harvard Law Review* is rarefied intellectual territory for anybody. Very few political candidates have that in their résumé.

That launched his career automatically, instantly. Offers came in from publishers to write books. His first memoir came from that achievement. The publishers said, "You became the editor of the *Harvard Law Review* and you're black too? Here's a book contract."

It was these two qualities, his natural talent and his separation from affirmative action, that made Barack Obama the first black in American history to plausibly run for the presidency. That is to say, here was somebody who was really in the game, who if things went his way would actually become the president of the United States. Jesse Jackson had run, Shirley Chisholm and Al Sharpton had also run. But everybody knew they were never going to win. They were never even going to get the nomination of their party and, of course, they didn't.

Barack Obama is the first to have a real chance at it. I think the first black in this position was Colin Powell who I firmly believe would have actually won the White House had he chosen to accept destiny when it came to his door, but he didn't. He demurred and so we'll never know.

So Obama is a phenomenon. The stars have aligned to give him a kind of magic and a presence that no other black in American history has ever had.

I'll move away from him for just a minute to talk a little about the existential circumstance of being a minority in any society. If you are a minority in any society, you are born into a collective experience of insecurity. We all are insecure as individuals. But if you are a minority, you also have a collective insecurity. You are born into a group that is nervous, wary and watchful as it makes its way in a society where it is outnumbered and vulnerable. And so there's going to be a different group psychology for minorities than for the majority. They're going to be looking at each other and thinking, "What my fellow minority does may jeopardize me. And so I've got to monitor him and watch him a lot more closely. I've got to make sure he doesn't step out of line, because if he does he's going to put me at risk." That's the Uncle Tom label, the idea that you are betraying the race.

Well, you don't have to do much in black America today to be an Uncle Tom. We are quick to label each other that way because we are trying to herd everybody into this singular position, this mask, this face that we're going to present to the larger society.

Minorities, by definition, have to wear masks. Inside the group, they figure out a mask that they're going to present to the larger society. Of course, the mask has a purpose: "They have more power than us, but we're going to present a mask that we hope will offset some of that power." Masks try to correct the imbalance of power between minorities and the majority.

So we're always trying to find out what kind of mask we're going to wear. Certainly, this goes back to slavery and segregation in black America. If you live in a society where everybody is more powerful than you, then you obviously are going to present yourself in a way that you hope will be strategic. And the result is that we rarely tell the larger society the truth.

One of my favorite lines in Ralph Ellison's *Invisible Man* comes as the invisible man is being kicked out of college by the college president because he has let a white man see the dark side of black life in Alabama. So the president calls him into his office and he says, "Listen, every nigger in the cotton patch knows you're supposed to lie to a white man. How did you get this stupid?" And then, of course, he says, "Well, you're so stupid I can't afford to have you around here." And he sends him away because he was naïve enough to tell a white man the truth—an unforgivable sin.

There are two great masks in black American history, I believe. One is called "challenging." The other is called "bargaining." The challenging mask appears when blacks stand before whites and they say, "I know you are a racist.

You know you are a racist. History proves that you are a racist. Now, you must prove to me that you're not one and here's what I want you to do. I want you to give me affirmative action. I want..." and there's a long laundry list of demands that are then made.

Challengers? The great ones at the moment are Jesse Jackson and Al Sharpton, who are always saying, "I start with the presumption that you're racist. You prove to me that you're not a racist." Well, these are extremely annoying figures in American life because it's painful and disconcerting to meet someone who doubts your moral character just on the basis of the color of your skin.

"You don't know I'm a racist." "Yes, I do." It's that sort of Kafkaesque accusation where the accusation becomes the truth. Then whites frantically try to prove to the Jesse Jacksons of the world that they're not racist—to the point of several billion dollars: $750 million from Texaco, $750 million from Toyota, $400 million from Coca Cola.

The other mask is much more effective for the most part. Bargainers always say to mainstream America, "I will never rub your face in America's odious history of racism. I will never presume that you a racist, if you never use my race against me." Fair deal.

Most white Americans, under the pressure of white guilt, are ever so happy to take that bargain. "Oh, thank you. A black who is going to give me the benefit of the doubt, who's not going to presume that I'm immoral, racist and so forth, but who's going to presume that I'm a decent person before I do anything."

That leads to what I call the gratitude factor. Toward blacks who bargain, whites then have an attitude of, "Oh, thank you. I'm so grateful that I'm going to be given a chance to be a decent person. I don't want to be seen as a racist. I'm not one. I'm so grateful." The gratitude factor rebounds to the benefit of the bargainer, who is then probably going to be held in higher esteem than they otherwise would be.

There have always been great bargainers. One of the first famous ones in the twentieth century was Louis Armstrong, who came along at a time when Jim Crow was entrenching itself. This was a virulently racist society. On the other hand, Louis Armstrong was a genius, was in every way a musical genius. His talent took him out into the larger world.

Well, how do you go out into the larger world that hates people of your color, that sees you as inferior, that despises you, and make a living as a musician? Well, here's what he did. He adapted an exaggerated grin. He always had a white handkerchief around his trumpet. He was always sweating. He bowed way too much, too deeply, too often.

In other words, what Louis Armstrong said is, "I know you people see me as inferior. I'm going to go along with that. I'm going to give you a little gesture of my inferiority, just to put you at ease, just so you will let me come in this hotel ballroom and play my music." That was the bargain he had to make in a racist society. It worked very well. People fell in love with Louis. Virulent segregationists loved Louis Armstrong.

The tragedy, of course, is that a black man of that level of genius, who virtually invented jazz, invented the jazz solo, had to make that offering of inferiority in order to be successful, in order to practice his art. God bless Louis Armstrong. When I was a kid, we held him up—but as I say, the tragedy was that he lived into the era of Miles Davis.

Miles Davis wore a mask too, and it was the exact opposite. He turned his back on the audience. He wouldn't speak. He didn't want even liner notes on his albums. His attitude was, "I'm not an entertainer. I'm an artist." His mask worked well too because, again, this was after World War II. Integration was beginning to happen. America was beginning to acknowledge its history of racism and what an honor it was to go to a nightclub and be cursed out by Miles Davis.

A friend of mine in Monterey is a jazz nut, and every time I see him I hear the story of him being cursed out at Shelly's Manhole back in the sixties by Miles Davis. It's one of the great moments of the man's life.

Well, again we see a mask that was designed, that was calculated, that was based on a reading of white Americans and where they were at, what they really wanted. And what genius on Miles's part. He knew white America had changed. He knew they wanted now to think of themselves as liberal and sophisticated. "So I'll curse them out. They'll really dig it." It worked.

Well, those masks still pertain today. The great bargainer of our time is Oprah Winfrey, who's an absolute genius at it. Before her, there was Bill Cosby in the eighties with *The Cosby Show*. Bill Cosby said, "If you watch my family show every week, I will not embarrass you. I will not shame you. You can watch it in comfort. Do not hold my race against me. I won't hold yours against you." It was a wonderful bargain.

You can always tell bargainers because they sell things very well. People love to put them in commercials. Bill Cosby sold mountains of Jell-O. With Oprah Winfrey, you know every writer longs to have an Oprah sticker on their book. It's just an automatic bestseller. Whatever Oprah says read, people read by the millions.

What happens with bargainers like that, and Oprah is again a good example, is that they tap the gratitude factor in white Americans. White Americans are proud of the fact that they like Oprah Winfrey. That's something you can brag about, that you can feel good about. You can say, "This is evidence that I'm not racist, that the stigma that history tries to put on me is not true. I like Oprah Winfrey. I respect her. I'd love to be her friend. I'd love to know her." And Oprah then respects her audience back.

So over time, a kind of reciprocity develops between the bargainer and white Americans. And that reciprocity intensifies in someone as famous as Oprah Winfrey and it gets to the point where they become what I call iconic Negroes.

An iconic Negro is sort of a super bargainer. You feel sorry for people who have to compete with them. Poor Phil Donahue had to compete with Oprah. He had no chance against somebody who has that kind of reciprocity with Americans. Tiger Woods is another example of someone who is a kind of iconic Negro. Michael Jordan, to some extent, is the same way. These people are obviously very talented, but there's also a reciprocity between them and America and it works very well.

I mentioned all this because Barack Obama is the first person who has tried to take the iconic Negro archetype into politics, into the dirty, muddy, back-alley business of American politics. That's the gamble that surrounds Barack Obama.

In America you frequently see "Oprah for President" bumper stickers. But Oprah's not really going to run, not really going to risk all that money on something as lowly as the presidency.

But Barack Obama is doing precisely that. The question is, "Will that model work? Will that bargaining mask—and it is a mask—work?" I think a lot of the appeal of Barack Obama comes from the fact that he is a natural bargainer. Even his interracial background plays a role in that.

He comes from a white mother and a black father, an African father. Whites instinctively know that if he has got a white mother, they can think, "How much is he really going to beat me up with that racist stigma? Because he knows that all white people are not racist." That's a great source of appeal. That's something that makes him much more endearing as a bargainer.

This is his charm, his charisma. He makes whites feel comfortable and hopeful. So he seems to be a transformative political figure, someone who might take America beyond its racial tragedy. He's the guy who might deliver us.

But there's another side to Barack Obama. And again, there's so much gratitude factor at work surrounding him that he becomes almost invisible. It's very difficult to see the real guy. The real man is somebody who was abandoned by his father, almost immediately. He never knew his father. He had met him for two weeks when he was ten. Like many people, one of the driving forces of his life was to conjure this grand image of his father and emulate it, and this propelled him forward. Yet he's driven by a kind of emptiness inside himself because there was, in fact, no father there.

Of course, his father was black and so, if the father was absent, so was the black identity. Here he was, a black kid being raised by a white mother and white grandparents in a white neighborhood in Hawaii. When he was around blacks, they teased him. "You're not really black. You speak standard English and that's not black."

From the very beginning, on the deepest psychic level, Obama has been driven by the need to get to know his father. Yet when he finally learns who his father really was, he is shattered. The man was a drunk. He was a ne'er-do-well. He had several families, children from several different women. He supported absolutely none of them. He failed in his career. And so Obama endured a real, almost psychic, collapse when he learned that this man who he thought was like Martin Luther King was really a rather tragic figure.

He then focused on establishing his black identity even more intensely. The question circling Obama has been, "Is he black enough?" But what does it mean if you're black enough?

Well, ideally it means that there's a kind of transparency; that when people see you, they see blackness. So you are one and the same thing; if you see a drug dealer on the corner who has got the sort of hip-hop regalia on, that's a black guy. There's a human being in there, but what we see is blackness.

Obama wants that on some level. He wants to be completely black. He wants the psychic solidity, the solidarity with other blacks that has always been denied him and is denied him to this day. The first thing Jesse does, when he wants to get Barack Obama mad, is say, "He acts like a white man. He's not really black." And Obama goes crazy because you're touching a very deep wound.

So he's in a very difficult position. On the one hand, his inner needs are to have a real transparent racial identity. On the other hand, America loves Barack Obama precisely for the opposite reason, precisely because he seems to be beyond the need for racial identity. In fact, it is very important to him. This is a man who spent twenty years in a black nationalist church on the south side of Chicago, a church his own mother could never feel comfortable in. So he is a divided man.

Again, on the one hand he appeals very much to whites but, when he does that, there's probably a voice inside him saying, "I'm not being black now. They're going to make me pay." And then, when he goes on the other side and he actually joins churches like this and goes every week and pretends to be super black he's saying, "What about my mother? What about my grand-father? What about my grandmother, the people I love, who raised me, who made me what I am?" They wouldn't be welcome in this church. The title of my book is *A Bound Man*.

How does a true self emerge from that kind of conflict? Very, very difficult. Every time he appeals to blacks—the black identity today being based on challenging—he has to be a challenger. So every time blacks like him, whites don't like him. They back away. "That's not the bargaining deal we bought with you. We don't want to see you in photo opportunities with Al Sharpton. We wanted you to be an anti–Al Sharpton."

If he then goes to whites and says, "Okay. I'm a bargainer and I'm a transformative figure. I'm going to take you beyond all this racial conflict and so forth," blacks stand back and say, "He's not really black. He's not black enough. He's a white man in disguise."

So he's bound again. Either way he goes, he loses. Is there a way out for Barack Obama? Yes. He has to become a man. He has to grow up and tell both white people and black people to go to hell. And he has to decide what he really believes and who he really is and what his convictions are and what he's willing to stand for and take his chances on.

Is he likely to do that? Sadly, I have to say there's not a lot of evidence to suggest that he is. A lifetime of being caught in a bind like this means that not much attention has been paid to an inner self.

So my own sense is that there is not much of a self there. He doesn't get angry very often, and that's not necessarily a good sign. Oftentimes when you get angry the real stuff comes out, and you get to know who you are a little bit. He never gets angry. And so, again, my sense is that he has paid a price.

Is he alone in this? No. I think in many ways much of my generation of black Americans—his generation of black Americans as well—have been stunted by this boundedness, this conflict between ourselves as individuals and our racial identity. Most of us, in the last forty years or so, have given much more emphasis to our racial identity than to ourselves as individuals and it has hurt us profoundly.

This is the weakest generation of black intellectuals in American history. You compare black writers today to people like Ralph Ellison and Richard Wright and James Baldwin, and we're a pretty paltry gang. I think a lot of it has had to do with the sacrifice of self, of individuality we have made simply to be able to say we're black. I hope we can move beyond this.

Has anybody of our generation moved beyond that? Yes. The freest black man in America, I believe, is Clarence Thomas, who wears absolutely no mask for anybody. He is his own man. Do you want to know what Clarence thinks? He'll tell you. You may or may not like it. He's a rare breed but, again, look at the price he pays. White people can't stand him. Black people can't stand him. Blacks say, "You're jeopardizing us." Whites say, "We can't stand next to you because, if we do, then we'll be seen as racist. So you're on your own, buddy."

And he is. And he's strong enough to carry that weight. But look at what sacrifices a minority has to make in modern America simply to be an individual, to think for themselves, to be who they are. That's the larger tragedy and, I think, the Achilles' heel of Barack Obama.

Q: Let's grant that a lot of the negatives that you referred to were associated with white support of the policies that you talked about. Taking the policy in itself, hasn't it produced better results than doing nothing, than leaving the layer of prejudice that exists in American society? Would you say that although this method had negatives, namely affirmative action, it did result in blacks moving up in ways that they wouldn't have if they had been just subject to the prejudice that existed anyway?

A: I knew we would somehow touch on affirmative action. Well, I simply could not disagree with you more.

I can't tell you the degree to which, as a human being, I loathe affirmative action. I grew up in segregation. I'd much rather live under segregation. I'd have a much better chance to be seen as an individual human being.

Affirmative action has not helped blacks in any way. It has deepened our psychology of dependency. It has subjected us to an experience of failure in every important university in the United States, all across the Ivy League where affirmative action is practiced assiduously. Go to any academic department and at the very bottom you'll find all the black students.

You'll find them terrorized, because they're unprepared, unable to compete. The term I use for it is they "recompose" that anxiety into the idea that they're really being oppressed by racism. So they believe in racism far more than I did, having grown up in segregation. I talk to these students on college campuses today and they tell me racism is around every corner. It's structural. It's systemic. I see opportunity everywhere, but to defend the failure, defend themselves from the sense of failure that affirmative action subjects them to, they have to scapegoat racism and that's what they do.

They're stigmatized for the rest of their entire lives with affirmative action. Every man, woman and child of my generation and younger is stigmatized with this odious white policy of paternalism.

Affirmative action was imposed on blacks. We never got to raise our hand and say, "I don't want it. I want to compete with everybody."

All of this so that the institutions can dissociate themselves from their reputation as racist. So who's benefiting from this? There's a new study out by the UCLA Professor Sanders that says only 25 percent of blacks who go to law school ever become lawyers. They flunk the bar exam at five times the rate that whites do. These are bright people who, if they were left alone to go into universities and colleges where they were able to compete, would have an experience of success, would like themselves, would grow up and would do just fine in society.

But white America insists that they be subjected to this kind of debilitating paternalism. It's the worst social policy in American history. It's just despicable and it makes my point about white liberal blindness, blindness to the human beings you are supposedly trying to help, and total white self-absorption. "All I care about is that I can say I support affirmative action because then people will say I'm not a racist. I'm happy."

No thought for what effect that's going to have on a race of people trying to crawl out of four centuries of oppression. You put them right back in the can again in the name of trying to help them. It's the worst thing that's happened to black Americans since the sixties.

We came into freedom in the sixties in the midst of a society that felt guilty about us, that was running from stigma itself, and so we began to feel that the thing to do was to invest in our identity, to be black. If you're black, you'll get further because whites will give you affirmative action. They'll give you welfare. They'll give you diversity. And so we bought that bill of goods and we put our emphasis on identity.

The tragedy is that most blacks today do wear masks, and Clarence Thomas is an exception. Certainly, most blacks who have become well known are not willing to take that kind of a risk. Oprah Winfrey is a perfect example. Suppose Oprah took her mask off and said, "You know what I really think? I don't think racism is that bad. I think we as blacks could do a whole lot better if we took more responsibility for ourselves."

She would no longer be an iconic Negro. She would lose her glamour. Whites would say, "I don't want to stand next to you because I will be called a racist." Bill Cosby lost his status as an iconic Negro because he asked blacks to take more responsibility.

Q: I'm just wondering where you place yourself, from a professional perspective, on the continuum between the challengers and the bargainers?
A: That's a good and fair question. By the mid-eighties, when I began to seriously write on race relations, I had to take all the masks off and write as Shelby Steele, and no one else. I don't speak for anybody else. I certainly don't speak for any race. I said exactly what I really thought and felt as an individual. Within two years I lost every single friend I had, every one. I was no longer welcome on my university campus and left.

So I have enormous empathy for blacks who don't want to take that mask off. Maybe I was selfish. I knew one thing: you couldn't be a very good writer if you were wearing a mask. People don't come to your work to see a mask. They come to see what you really think.

It was only when I took the mask off that I was then able to see what the mask had been, that I had bargained. I talk about it in my books. When I was in college, I wore an Afro as big as a bush. I was Mr. Militant, a real challenger and while growing up I probably did more bargaining. I didn't like it very much.

But I wanted to be a writer and a writer has to have a degree of authenticity. I finally just told the world what I thought. I feel enormously free today. Most blacks I know are not. That's my reward. I may have lost a lot of friends. I may be a pariah in some quarters, but I'm a very relaxed person inside, more so than I ever was before, when every time I stepped on campus, I had to play some role and fight for things like affirmative action that disgusted me and play along with those kinds of games. I don't have to do that any more.

Q: Do you think that Oprah made Obama "black" again by her endorsement and the fundraiser and all of the money that came from the blacks?

Secondly, there are blacks that support the Clintons and blacks that support Barack Obama. Could you ever see a merge of those two as this race winds down?

A: It's an interesting question. I think Oprah's too much of a bargainer to really have the power to make Barack black. The only one who can make him black is a challenger. If Jesse Jackson says he's black, he's black. If Al Sharpton says he's black, he's black and he's black enough.

Oprah is, you know, sort of above the fray. She's a super bargainer and so she doesn't have the moral authority. The blacks who have moral authority are challengers. They're the ones who can vet whites as innocent. You know, when

Don Imus made his big mistake on radio, who was the first black he ran to? Not Colin Powell or Condoleezza Rice, but Al Sharpton because Al Sharpton's a challenger and therefore he has the moral authority to vet him, to say he's decent or not. There was Don Imus at his feet.

Oprah doesn't have that kind of moral authority among blacks. She has got, certainly, the elite, wealthy Hollywood set to contribute a lot of money and so forth and she has every right to do that. I don't think she hurts him either, but I don't think she helps very much.

The conflict among blacks between Hillary and Barack is interesting. There are all kinds of ways to look at that. You know, Hillary and Bill Clinton have a huge machine that has been around for decades, and they are owed all sorts of things by all sorts of people and so there's just regular old politics going on. Most blacks sort of see that. You know, the Charles Rangels of the world, the black caucus, they sort of say, "I like Barack, good guy, but here's my bread and butter," and so, much of the leadership is probably in support of Hillary Clinton for that reason.

Barack is the new guy on the street. He has got nothing particularly valuable to offer them. Having said that, on election day if Barack Obama's name is on the ballot and Hillary Clinton's name is on the ballot, my guess is most blacks will vote for Barack Obama. There's too strong an identity there to say, "Well, okay. This is **the first** chance I have in my whole life ever to vote for **a black man** but I'm going to vote for a white woman." So I think on election day, Barack will do well among blacks.

Q: Does Condoleezza Rice have a mask?
A: Condoleezza Rice is a good example of a black who does not have much of a mask at all and pays the price for it, is satirized and called every name in the book. If they are a pariah, they probably don't wear a mask.

Q: Is there something that the black civil rights movement can learn from the women's movement and vice versa?
A: I'll have to think about that. That sounds like a book assignment there. I'm sure there is.

I think both of those movements after the sixties, after the initial victories of the women's movement as well as the black movement, became victim-focused movements, hurt themselves. When you say, "My legitimacy in American life is my victimization as a woman or as a black," well, you might get a short-term gain but where are you going to get in the long run? And how long can you hold that ground? So I think both movements hurt themselves.

You know, when you're talking about blacks, you're talking about people who were put upon for four centuries, who were denied everything, education, who came into freedom—there's no other word for it—backward. How could you go through four centuries of oppression and be au courant and competitive with other groups?

That wasn't true to the same degree for women. Women too were put upon, they didn't have opportunities in the same way, and I think women were victimized, but I don't think it was to the same degree. The proof of that is that they have done infinitely better. One of the big gripes blacks have against affirmative action is that women are about 80 percent of the beneficiaries of affirmative action because they were better educated. They were educated with their brothers. They had opportunities that certainly blacks never had, and so they have done better all across the board.

It is a fact. It doesn't mean that they're not victimized. I don't want to take anybody's victimization away from them. God forbid. You have a right to your victimization. I've got a right to mine. But it's a complex picture and that's one of the big differences between the two movements, it seems to me.

ON THE DEMOCRATIC LEADERSHIP RACE
James Carville
February 6, 2008

JAMES CARVILLE—dubbed the "Ragin' Cajun"—was President Bill Clinton's former campaign manager, and, in this lecture, comes out firing on all eight cylinders. Carville sees the Republicans as a party of "old white guys, and really old white guys." According to his wife, the Republican adviser, Mary Maitland, "Democrats fall in love, Republicans fall in line."

Carville points out that Obama and Hillary represent two aspects of the Democratic party: Party A and Party B. Obama appeals to Party A: the more educated, wealthy and sophisticated voter, while Hillary supporters fall in the Party B category: generally older, union-based and with less formal education. Carville also illustrates the contradiction that black Americans were traditionally attracted to party B rather than party A. On the policy side, Carville admits there's not much difference between the two candidates. The difference is all style.

Although technically not an adviser to Hillary Clinton's campaign, Carville thinks it was a mistake not to go negative early in the race for the democratic leadership. But he saw all that change after Super Tuesday and now predicts a ruthless race. "There's a lot more getting ready to happen," he says. "This thing is going to keep on giving. It ain't going to stop."

I'M GOING TO DO something I don't normally do. I'm going to say something nice about President Bush. This summer he was at his daddy's place at Kennebunkport with Nicolas Sarkozy, the French president. (I'm French, actually. My people are from Canada and I can say this, sometimes we can be kind of annoying.) Bush had had enough of the French and he looked Sarkozy right in the eye and said, "You know, the problem with you French is you don't have a word for entrepreneur."

Which reminds me of the other great Republican linguist, Dan Quayle, who once went to Venezuela and gave a speech at the Caracas Chamber of Commerce. He proclaimed that he loved Latin America and he loved the people of Latin America and his great regret in life was that he never learned to speak Latin.

My wife, Mary Maitland, is a publisher of a conservative book line. I'm very proud of her. She had four New York Times bestsellers at one time, which is almost unprecedented—and she has just signed Karl Rove's new book. But the thing I'm excited about is that she has got a new Harry Potter book. It's called *Harry Potter and the*

Search for the Illegal Immigrant by Lou Dobbs.

I have to tell you, I'm an unbelievable admirer of Canada for one simple reason. Any people that are so self-confident about themselves that they actually have a leaf for their national symbol are people to be admired. Everybody else has to have an eagle or a lion or a bear. You show your self-confidence and self-esteem with a simple leaf. That's a really cool thing. And every time a leaf falls on my head, I think of Canada.

I'll give you my thoughts about the American election and they are this: Oh, my God.

This election is not historical. It's not unimaginable and it's not transformational. This election is incomprehensible. What you're seeing in this election year has no precedent anywhere in our history. In this cycle, we've had the first credible woman run for president, the first credible African American, the first Hispanic, the first Italian American. We've had people that have been married twice run for president. And the first Mormon. I always point out to my Republican friends, of all their major candidates, Fred Thompson, Rudy Giuliani, Mitt Romney, John McCain, the only one married once was the Mormon, which is pretty remarkable when you think of it.

The last time that the Republican party didn't have an obvious designated front-runner was in 1940, with Wendell Willkie. It has been that long since we have had a nominating process this open.

ON THE DEMOCRATIC LEADERSHIP RACE

The last time we had an election in the United States where there was not a sitting president or vice-president—with the exception of 1952 when Eisenhower ran, whom both parties wanted to run—was 1928. For that fact alone, this election year is remarkable.

The amount of money that has been raised is not even unprecedented. I can say it's incomprehensible. The turnout is incomprehensible. We're seeing in some places 100 percent increases in turnout, particularly on the Democratic side. And these are just the primaries.

Consider that eight million people watched the last Democratic debate. That's politicians talking to each other on cable TV. Eight million people. Worldwide wrestling can only get three million. What you're seeing is something so remarkable that we're all just trying to digest what's happening.

There are all of these fascinating stories. You've had the biggest disaster in American presidential history, the Rudy Giuliani campaign. We've had the first candidate in the history of U.S. politics to test positive for Ambien, Fred Thompson. The guy ran for president and never woke up. It's remarkable that something like that could happen.

Now, we'll talk a little bit about the Republicans and then I'm going to talk more about the Democrats, not just because I'm a Democrat but because that's the really interesting story. The Republicans' only conflict is in the Republican party. The Democrats have got the African

American vote and we've got the educated white women vote. We also have the Hispanic and youth vote. In the Republican party, the argument is between old white guys and really old white guys. But remember what I said at the beginning of my remarks about how the Republicans always have a designated front-runner and they always get behind him. My wife has a brilliant line that she uses that's true: "Democrats fall in love. Republicans fall in line."

But the problem is that they're not falling in line. They don't know whether to wind their butts or scratch their watch. They're saying, "Gee, we're kind of stuck with McCain," Rush Limbaugh is furious, they're all going nuts out there—and it's very confusing. If you're a Republican, you're saying, "Damn, Arthur. What line are we getting in here?" and "We've all got to get behind somebody." And it just goes on and on. Because, you see, all little families have little secrets and the Republican have their little secret.

The internal squabble with the Republicans is that you've got three distinct divisions in the U.S. Republican party. The first is what I call the God-guns kind of Republicans: more God, more guns. You know the type. Then you have the economic conservatives, the ones who say, "Get out of my way. Don't tax me. Don't regulate me. Let me pollute the hell out of everybody and make all the money I can." And finally you have the national defense muscular military foreign policy wonks, the ones who say, "Rah, rah, ree. Kick them in the knee. Rah, rah, rass. Kick them in the other knee."

And these three groups are having a hard time coming together. Now, the amazing thing is that there's no kind of front-runner for everybody to fall in line behind. There's a prototype of a classic Republican front-runner in the U.S., twice governor of a large swing state, very popular, speaks Spanish, in cool with the social conservatives, great with the business community and a great fundraiser. His name is Jeb Bush. If his name was Jeb Smith, there wouldn't be a race at all and we wouldn't have had all these ugly little family squabbles. Everybody would have fallen in line. But they didn't. Now they've got a really old white guy that a lot of the other white guys don't like.

On the Democratic side, we also have our little squabbles and secrets. There are basically two kinds of Democrats in the United States. Let's just say Party A tends to be more affluent, heavily female, educated, suburban, reform oriented. It's a big part of the Democratic party. Think of Paul Tsongas, Bill Bradley, and Eugene McCarthy. All had lots of women supporting them.

Then you have Party B, people who look to the federal government to soften the harder edges of capitalism with unemployment insurance, Medicare, social security, heating oil assistance, and so on. This group tends to be more downscale; more urban than suburban.

Now, Barack Obama clearly represents Party A. Hillary

Clinton is more Party B. She speaks more about people struggling in the middle class. Obama speaks in a lofty kind of "process" way. However, the beautiful thing here is that you have a contradiction within a contradiction because African Americans, who always reside in Party A, are now voting for the candidate in Party B and Party A voters are also voting for the candidate of Party B. The reason the race is so unpredictable is that you have the contradiction but then you have the contradiction within the contradiction.

I can't tell you exactly what's going to happen, but I can tell you this. There's a lot more that's going to happen. This thing is going to keep on giving. It ain't going to stop.

The fascinating thing on the Democratic side is that the policy differences between Clinton and Obama are minimal. Her health care plan is more comprehensive than his, but they both don't like global warming. They both like pro-choice and they both want to get us out of Iraq.

The real difference is the argument. Obama's process argument is, "I can circumvent the system. If the system's broke, I can go over the system to get what you want done." Hillary's message is, "I'm one tough woman. I'll cut through the system and make them do what you want me to make them do."

So you have one person saying, "I can circumvent the system," and the other person saying, "I can manipulate the system." And if you watch them speak, you can see that. It's a fascinating time in the Democratic party.

Let me tell you what I think is going on. George Will said in the year 2000, "It was good to be alive in America at the end of the first, but not last, American century." Charles Krauthammer, who's a big prominent neocon, said in 2000, "No other nation has exercised such military, economic, and cultural and diplomatic reach since Rome. America bestrides the world like a colossus." Friends, it's seven years later. Just seven years, and if somebody said that today, they would be laughed out of this room.

The average American understands that. They get it. They know what has happened to their income. They know what has happened to the prestige of their country. They know what has happened to the deficit. They know what has happened to their currency. They know what has happened to their military. They know it. That's what's driving this.

It has been seven years. We generally think of history in sweeps or as in Edward Gibbon's *The Decline and Fall of the Roman Empire*. This has been something that has happened fast. Now, that's the bad news.

The good news is that we understand that. And what you're seeing is people, in their own way, through the political system, trying to deal with it. That's why you're really seeing this enormous level of interest.

Q: Can Obama win the presidency? What is at stake—since you already said there's not that much difference between the policies of the two?

A: The country really does not want to elect another Republican. What I tell my audiences is, "For all you Democrats out there, I've got great news for you. We have to talk our way out of winning this election. And for all you Republicans, I have great news for you. Don't worry, we're perfectly capable of doing that."

Obama could win. And the Republican party is held in the lowest esteem in modern history of any political party. But, you know, it will be a very tough campaign. But sure, absolutely he could win.

Q: Is there a possibility that Obama and Clinton could be on the same ticket?

A: Sure. Historically we saw it with Kennedy and Johnson, Reagan and Bush, Kerry and Edwards. Democrats are pretty satisfied with their choice. They like both of them. The idea that this has been a divisive campaign is not particularly true at all. In fact, it's a little wussified for me.

Look, I think that they've got to get after each other. Obama, if he wins, hasn't taken a punch and, believe me, the Republicans are going to throw them. And they're pretty good at it.

Q: If you were going to run a campaign for the Democrats, who would you rather be running it for, Clinton or Obama?
A: I'd rather run it for Clinton because I know her and I love her. Politics is personal to me. But I'll support whomever the Democratic nominee is.

Q: Do you think that McCain can beat Hillary because of her negatives and that Obama can beat McCain because he can appeal to something broader and to younger voters?
A: I remember in a Gallup poll, John Kerry was 14 points up on Bush in March of '04. I would be very skeptical of using a poll right now because campaigns play out. Right now it's a fact that if you took a poll most would show Obama running a little ahead of McCain. Most polls show Hillary running a little bit behind.

We saw what happened to the polls in New Hampshire. So if the election were held tomorrow, Obama would be a stronger general election candidate. But it's not. It's going to be held in November. I'll give you the argument to the contrary.

It is that Obama has never been attacked. He has only three years' experience in the Senate and the Republicans will eat him alive. Every negative about Hillary is already known. It's battle-worn, tested. What are they going to say? She can come back. That will be much more effective.

Q: You describe a country dealing with the prospect of national decline: i.e., environmental degradation, climate change, global warming. How would you handle these issues as a campaign advisor?

A: I think that there's probably no country on earth that's more affected by climate change than Canada. But you have to create drama. You have to create a narrative. You can't just let go. There has to be a clock, like in *High Noon*. You're always running against the clock. I think in the U.S. the people are much ahead of the government on this.

You also have to create a villain. Every story has to have a narrative, a conflict if you will. If the party wants to do that, then there has to be an impediment to action. And that impediment is the Republican party.

Q: In 1992, you said, "It's the economy, stupid." So what it is now? What are the American people trying to express about their values in this election?

A: Americans are seeing their standard of living starting to slip away. They see their national prestige decline. They see the budget deficit growing. What I would say is it's time to get control of things; things have been out of control for too long. I think that's what people feel. And they feel like their country doesn't have control over what happens in the world and they don't have control over what happens in their lives.

Now, on a campaign, you certainly couldn't go out and

say, "We're a country in decline." That's why Obama says, "I can circumvent it and we can be great again and it's just the politicians and the partisanships that are standing in the way." Or as Clinton says, "I'm tough enough and I'll make us great again by cutting through and slapping these politicians around because I'm a lot tougher than they are." No one is going to run for office and say, "Gee, our country is declining," because people know it but they want a way out.

That's why Roosevelt said, "The only thing we have to fear is fear itself." The loss of control has really got people in great angst. I would say it's about a loss of control.

Q: I perceive the American media, especially beginning with Iowa in particular, have had nothing good to say about Hillary Clinton. They are hanging on to Obama's coattails. I would like to see if you agree with that analysis.
A: I do.

Q: And can you tell me why that is?
A: First of all, it depends on the kind of reporter. The press think Obama's campaign is something new and fresh and different and it would be a great story. And if Hillary wins, it will be, "We covered this story eight years in the White House. We have decided that we want a fresh story, so we'll do everything we can to get our fresh story." That's really not their role, but that's kind of what they've decided.

Hillary started out with a pretty dumb strategy that her

win was inevitable, that they would win. That has been abandoned, thank God. I think the press recoiled from that also. But they decided very early that they were tired of the Clinton story; they wanted another story and that was what's behind it.

Q: Some argue that the U.S. government is effectively bankrupt, given their assets and liabilities. Will this be a campaign issue or will the candidates just punt the football forward and figure they'll solve it later?
A: They'll punt the football forward and figure out how to solve it later. Look, they've got to refigure this thing. Canada has universal health care for everyone, but it's not breaking your country. Why do we have forty-nine million uninsured people and it's breaking us? Because we're spending 16 percent of our GDP and you're spending 8 percent. I'm not an economist, but if you're spending 16 percent of your GDP over a period of time as compared to 8 percent it's going to bite you on the ass. And that's the kind of simple answer to it.

But if you're covering everybody at half the cost, we should look at universal health care. And, by the way, while we're spending 16 percent of our GDP on health care, we spend more on our military than the next nine nations in the world combined.

On military spending, the next president may have to say, "Look, everybody has got to get a little skin in this game, not just us." Our ability to just sit there and be wealthy enough to do all of the things that we are accustomed to do is a challenge. It's catching up with us.

I think people are hoping the next president has the ability to bring that up and have people see that, and I think they will. And the demographics are not working well for us for the next twenty or thirty years.

Q: We do not know everything about Barack Obama. When and if there is something to be known which would not be favorable, when would that come out?
A: Look, there's something negative on everybody. They like the idea of, "Here's some kind of fresh meat in the game," if you will. The Republicans will come out with stuff that we'll never know about. It will all come to pass in the general election. He'll have a pretty good vetting before this is over, if he is the nominee.

Q: Would the Democratic party allow themselves to be rent apart in this way, if there were something negative and he was going to be the candidate? Would that internecine battle happen beforehand?
A: No, it won't happen. The Democrats are wusses. They say: "We don't like people to go negative. They should only talk about the issues and I don't like when they attack each other. It just makes me nervous. My herbal tea just doesn't sit well."

I'm more of the school of, "Let them air it out a little bit. It's not going to kill anybody." I can be for either one, but call him (Obama) an upstart and call her (Hilary) an old hag.

I think that a little rough-and-tumble in politics is not something that's all that terrible. If he thinks that dealing with Hillary Clinton is tough—"May I introduce you to Mr. Vladimir Putin, Senator Obama? He ain't exactly the nicest guy in the world. And this is Mr. Ahmadinejad and he's certainly not a lovely man."

The single stupidest thing ever said by an elected official in this century is when Bush said, "I looked into Vladimir Putin's eyes and I saw the soul of a good man." And he is a lot of things, but a good man ain't one of them. The KGB didn't produce a lot of soft people.

Q: It is hard to believe Americans will elect a President with only three years' experience in the Senate. Can you comment?
A: Look, I'll give you the converse here. Obama's a talented guy. He could be a quick study. He's a good speaker. But you're right, that is a concern. And this is a classic conflict: he wants to circumvent the process. She wants to cut through it.

His message is classic inspiration. Hers is classic perspiration. Obama: "I will inspire you. I will inspire us to do great things." Clinton: "I will work my ass off to get great things done." So many people, particularly women, are saying, "You know what? I know what she's going through. I know what she's up against." She's orderly. She's methodical. She's smart. She'll go about it this way.

But then Obama says, "I don't lead. I don't do stuff with my desk. I lose things." You know, maybe that's what we need, maybe that's not, but they're two completely different people. They're not ideologically different. It's not that one is a white woman and one is an African American male. That's not what I'm talking about.

They're two different people in their approach to the job. They're two different people in the way that they approach things. And it is just a classic confrontation of inspiration and perspiration.

You say to yourself, "We know that inspiration will work better in the first three months, but the question is what works best for the first three years." And I don't know. But that's the fundamental clash that's going on in American politics.

AN ELECTION FOR THE AGES
David Gergen
May 1, 2008

DAVID GERGEN, CNN COMMENTATOR, professor at the Kennedy School of Government at Harvard and bipartisan pundit, wrapped things up by saying Republican candidate Senator John McCain is starting to appeal to Reagan Democrats disillusioned with the internecine battle in the Democratic party. But he reminds us that Americans want out of the war in Iraq and a better economy, and that still bodes well for the Democrats in November. Still, he argues, there's no question the Democrats look much weaker than they did when this race started.

I HAVE BEEN ASKED to address the topics of American politics and where we find ourselves leading up the election in November. I must tell you, though, that I've been around this track probably too long. This is my tenth presidential campaign—my tenth presidential campaign! I started out working in the trenches for candidates, and more recently have been in studios, kibitzing from the sidelines.

So here we are, ten campaigns later, and I'm absolutely fascinated, riveted, by this race. It is the most interesting, most exciting race we've had in half a century in the United States. I would add that it's also probably the most important election we've had in half a century. And for me, the serious question about this race is not who wins, but can the winner govern? Can the winner lead?

I honestly believe that the next president will face the toughest challenges of any new president in more than half a century. You have to go all the way back to Franklin Roosevelt in March of 1933 to find a president who inherited a more daunting set of challenges. Many of the problems we're facing now have been around for a long,

long time, but we've been unable to solve them. We have delayed, we've been in denial, we've been divided. Our society—and Canada to a significant degree, but our society far more—has found it almost impossible, for example, to reach agreement on a comprehensive energy plan that also is respectful of the environment. We just haven't done it. I was there in the early 1970s when OPEC raised its head and tried to strangle the world economy, and I wrote some of those early presidential speeches calling for energy independence. That was our battle cry, back in the early 1970s. Well, those speeches were very successful, weren't they? We're about twice as dependent today as we were then!

But energy is only one of several issues that have been kicking around for a long, long time. And now the bills are coming due and we have to act. We no longer have the luxury of arguing. The time has come for action. And whether the United States is going to be up to that while also dealing with the other myriad issues that are on the table—like nuclear proliferation, Iran, Iraq, and all the rest—is very much open to question.

In my judgment, each of the individuals now running for president would make a very fine chief executive in ordinary times. I think we're blessed indeed in this race to have winnowed the field down to three candidates who would each, if elected, break a record. We have a former POW. We've got a woman. We've got an African American. And they're all people of character. They're all people of better judgment than the incumbent. They're all people who I think have a lot of drive. But it's not yet clear to me that any one of them can rise to the heights that are going to be needed. I don't think we need ordinary leadership in the next four to eight years. I think we need extraordinary leadership. And one of the things this campaign must do is help us sort out who can be extraordinary. It's a testing of the candidates, a chance for us to get a better sense of who these people are.

As bumpy and as difficult as these last few weeks have been for Barack Obama, for example, at least he's being tested in a very public way, and we're getting a better sense of who this man is. Does he have the steel? Does he have the inner toughness, that is ultimately required in this job? I don't think we have the definitive answer yet, but we may be getting close. In some ways, this long campaign has been good for all of us.

Now, where are we with the race? I'd like to spend a bit of time on where the race may be going, where it may not be going, and the challenges that are ahead.

This is a race that, according to all historical lessons, should be won by the Democrats by somewhere between five and ten points, which would be a near landslide. We have a situation in which one party has held the White House for eight years, and in which the incumbent is not running. We've had five such elections since the 1950s. In four of those elections, the out-of-power party has won. Only when Reagan was president did the "in" party win again, and that's because Reagan was so popular at the end of his presidency that the next election, when George Bush Sr. won, was in effect a referendum on Reagan.

Historically, then, this should be a lay down. But you've got other factors to add into the mix—factors that work in the Democrats' favor. This particular president, for example, has been such a huge disappointment that many people who voted for him eight years ago have moved from a sense of disappointment to befuddlement to resentment to deep anger about what he is doing to some of the institutions that we've watched other presidents labor hard to build. He's ripped apart relationships, destroyed America's good reputation in so many parts of the world, and has left unattended so many problems that demanded our attention. And then there are the wars he's going to leave behind.

There's a survey out now that says only 27 percent of the country approves of Bush's Republicans. Only 21 percent approves of his economic policies. And 73 percent of the country—a very, very high number—believes that the country is on the wrong track. We haven't seen numbers like these since the end of the last Bush One administration, which brought Clinton into office.

So what you have, then, is a set up that calls for a Democratic victory. And if you think this is just temporary, that people are just angry about the war, it goes far deeper than that. Some observers both in the U.S. and abroad are very concerned about trade and the populism we see in America. I take this populism very seriously, and I think it does have repercussions and importance to Canada. But that populism is rooted in something deeper. We seem to be in the early stages of a fundamental change in Western economics. Globalization is driving up the rewards for those on top and driving down the returns for those in the middle or at the bottom. And the economic growth record under George W. Bush is the lowest since Dwight Eisenhower. We've had the lowest record of job increases since the Second World War. Under President Clinton poverty went down. Under President Bush poverty has gone up. Under President Clinton average income went up. Under George W. Bush it has gone down significantly. That has left a lot of scars. And it's left people feeling very, very pushed. It's one of the reasons we're seeing this populism. But it also has opened the door to a Democratic victory. And yet even with all these factors in play, we find that John McCain is running even—in a statistical dead heat with both Barack Obama and Hillary Clinton.

My own sense is that when a Democratic nominee does emerge, there is going to be a movement toward that Democrat and the party will then open an eight- to ten-point lead. And the big question is, can they hold it? It's not clear they can. But we're in an unnatural part of the campaign right now. For the Democrats this is sort of the nadir. The fight is very tough, very messy, very bloody. And McCain can be off, unscarred, standing above it all, unchallenged in many ways. I think when the real fight starts, you're going to find arguments being made that will make John McCain's job a lot tougher. I continue to believe the Democrats are likely to win this, but it's possible John McCain could win. I think the odds are about sixty-forty in the Democrats' favor, but those odds started out greater. Those odds have narrowed.

For the Democrats, then, this has been a totally unexpected battle. We all thought Hillary Clinton was going to close the deal back in February. *She* thought she was going to close the deal back in February. But for reasons that remain mysterious, she has run a lousy campaign. She may be ready to be president on Day One, but she was not ready to be a candidate on Day One. And that's surprising. I think even Bill Clinton shares that assessment. The Clintons were not prepared for the length of this campaign, or at least for how popular Barack Obama would turn out to be. I think when Clinton got into this she was so certain of winning that her team didn't plan it out beyond February 5. They weren't ready to go beyond Super Tuesday. They did not take the caucuses seriously. They thought they could just sweep the big states. I don't know who was doing the math, but it turns out the caucuses are pretty darn important when it comes to actually getting pledged delegates. And Obama, because he was such an underdog, started out with only 20 percent name recognition against this overwhelming favorite. He had to fight everywhere in order to have any chance at all.

Let's take a minute on the system—this peculiar system for counting the vote. On Super Tuesday, just to use one example, there were elections all across the country. One of those that we in the so-called "commentariat" kept our eye on was New Jersey—a big industrial state, a critical state in the overall scheme of things. And Hillary Clinton campaigned hard. She had John Corzine, the governor, campaigning hard for her. Barack went in and tried to compete, but he couldn't beat her. She won a significant victory—eight to ten points. So you would think she gets a rich harvest of delegates, right? Not when you win by eight to ten points. Delegates are awarded in an essentially proportional way, so she didn't end up with many more delegates than he did.

Meanwhile, on the same day, the state of Idaho has a caucus. Now almost nobody, unless you're a fisherman, goes to Idaho. Clinton didn't go to Idaho, but Obama did. He went out and campaigned in Idaho and he swept the caucuses by a huge margin. And when you allocated the delegates from the two states, Idaho and New Jersey together, he actually came out one delegate ahead.

The Clinton campaign hadn't figured that out. They conceded these caucuses, and that gave Obama a significant lead in pledged delegates, which has put Clinton in a very awkward situation. I think they "misunderestimated," to use a George Bush term, Barack's appeal. They didn't see it coming, and I think what we're seeing now is a lot of resentment within the Clinton campaign about this upstart. Why is he challenging us? We're the legitimate heirs. He hasn't earned this. There's a deep-seated feeling among the Clintons that Obama can't win, that he will be a threat to the future of the party, and that they have to stop him. That's their obligation: to stop him.

No one mistakes the fact that the Clintons think it's their obligation—and their right, their entitlement—to have the White House. And so in going after Obama recently, Clinton became a street fighter. Obama has tried to stay above it all, and as a result, she's made up some ground against him. But she's also hurt herself. She's driven up her own negatives even as she's driven up his.

There are a lot of people who look at this and say that a woman faces a double bind here. Of course, an African American male in the white culture of the United States will also be stereotyped, so let's address that first. Obama has had to fight against all the old myths, the racial prejudice and so forth that roll around out there. But once he does break out—once he shows the voters that he's not dangerous, that he's going to work in a partnership—suddenly they see him as acceptable.

I know many people who feel proud to have Obama in this race. I'm from the white South. I grew up in North Carolina. For me, this race has a quality of redemption about it. For many of us who come from the South, who bear a sense of guilt about our past, voting to put an African American in the White House is a powerful thing. It stirs me. It goes beyond the quality of the individual. As long as the person is qualified, that stirs me.

By contrast, I want to make a point about the double bind for a woman. The stereotype is that she's going to be a sort of "go along, get along" leader, a weak, nourishing, helpful partner, co-partner or lower partner. She won't take charge, and she's probably not up to the tough decisions that are required in the inner sanctums of government or corporate life. Therefore, she's probably not qualified. To break out of that stereotype, a woman has to show something else. She has to show strength and decisiveness. But now, of course, she's a bitch. And she's caught in that trap. Many, many women get caught in that trap. So the reaction to Hillary's fighting has been, "Well, it's okay that she fights, but I'm not comfortable with her in my living room."

And we need to take that seriously, because there's very much a living room test that goes into the selection of America's presidents. More than with any other position in our society, people apply a values and likability test to potential presidents. If they *like* you, they're much more willing to vote for you. "I like Ike" was the single most effective popular slogan in all of American political history. And his smile made a huge difference, as it did for Reagan. For many people, Clinton is tough but not likable. And that is getting in her way as she tries to close this deal.

And so here comes Obama out of nowhere—gifted oratorically, very smart, went to the Harvard Law School. While he was there a constitutional scholar named Larry Tribe—one of the foremost constitutional scholars in the country—was there too. And he's been telling people all about Barack—the first African American editor of the *Havard Law Review*, the smartest kid he ever taught. And that is working for Obama.

In recent times, however, we're seeing some things about Obama that we don't fully understand. He's going through a terrible vetting right now, and we're learning about some of the early associations he made that were, perhaps, mistakes. And Hillary got to him, tore him down some.

I had a friend who advised Obama very early on. Barack went to see this veteran of American politics—who has been in Washington, been in Chicago, and knows politics extremely well, knows the Clintons extremely well. And my friend told Barack, "Listen, the question is not whether you can take a punch, the question is whether you can throw a punch." I didn't understand that when I first heard it, but boy has it come back to help define what's going on now. There are a lot of people asking, can this guy throw a punch? Does he have what it takes to stand up to someone like Putin in a tough clinch? If he gets into it with Ahmadinejad, he may not be able to solve the problems just by talking. You may have to have somebody tougher at the table. And there are going to be a lot of situations where that kind of inner steel makes a big difference to leadership.

I think Obama's inspirational quality is marvelous, and the speech he gave after the first Reverend Wright episode broke was one of the best speeches since King's "I have a dream." It was so refreshing to have someone talk to us as if we're adults instead of having the cheesy, adolescent conversations we so often get in our national politics. But the question is still, is the guy tough enough to get the job done? Because there are times you can't make everybody come together around the same table and agree. There are times when some people lunge at you, times when you've got to be able to smack 'em down. And there are times that people, tough people, can become your enemies.

When Franklin Roosevelt was president he did a marvelous job rallying the country. He also acquired a great number of enemies. And in 1936, when he ran again, he said how proud he was to have these enemies. He liked the combat. He enjoyed the fisticuffs of politics. You have to enjoy the exercise of power. It's not just a question of getting there. The people who are best at this are the people who enjoy the exercise of power and also have strong values, and have a clear sense of what they want to achieve. And we don't know quite about the first part of this equation with Barack.

We are at a point where the big question of the moment is whether this preacher—this egomaniac, Jeremiah Wright—is going to cost Barack Obama the nomination. And I don't think any of us knows the answer.

But the Wright danger is serious. Let me tell you why it's a train wreck. Let's say that Clinton does well enough over the next few weeks to make it very, very clear that white America is not voting for Obama. If this happens, the Democrats are going to wind up with a nomination cycle in which she will be behind in terms of delegates, she will be behind in terms of votes cast, and she will be behind in terms of states won.

African Americans will come to the conversation about who ought to get the nomination with some serious and difficult questions. They're going to say that, for a century or more you've been telling us that if we want to get ahead in the United States we need to come to the table, play by the rules, and work hard. And if we're diligent and play by the rules, we'll be properly rewarded. Now, African Americans will say, "Okay, we played by the rules, we got more votes, more delegates and more states, and you're saying you're not going to give it to Barack because he's black? Is

AN ELECTION FOR THE AGES / 103

that what you're saying?" Can you imagine how poisonous that is for the Democratic party, which relies heavily on the black vote? It's a very, very dangerous game to play.

And then there's the youth vote, which is also vitally important. We've had a real problem with civic disengagement with our youth, and yet, a great number of young people who have not voted in the past have voted this time out. We haven't seen anything like this kind of youth turnout since Kennedy. I've had busloads of students from the Kennedy School go to Pennsylvania, go to Ohio. They're going to North Carolina, they're going to Indiana. They really are caught up in this race. For the first time in a long time, we have a lot of young people very, very excited about this game.

If you're running the Democratic party you know how important this is. You know that, historically, if someone between the ages of say 18 and 26 votes for you once, and then they vote for you or your party again four years later, they are likely to vote for your party most of their lives. One of the reasons that there are a lot of young people in the United States—in their thirties and forties—who are much more conservative than some of their colleagues is because of the Reagan influence. People who voted for Reagan twice have tended to remain pretty conservative.

So the Democrats have this chance with Obama to get people—young people—to vote Democratic. And if they get them a couple of times, it will be the basis for a new majority, a long-term majority. Are they going to throw out those young people? Young people are likely to turn very cynical if they think this is stolen from Obama. That's why this is a real problem, and why many, many Democrats fervently hope that Obama goes ahead and wraps this thing up. If it goes the other way, it's going to be a real mess.

I don't want to spend much time on McCain, but I will tell you he's riding high right now. People like him so much. There's no question he's the most likeable person in the race. He's the person you'd want to have dinner with first. He's fun, he's provocative, he's a little raunchy, he's irreverent, but he's got interesting values, and he comes from a long line of people who served with valor in the United States military. I was with John and Cindy McCain last summer. Three generations of McCains have been to the naval academy. And they've got a son in the naval academy now. He's the fourth-generation McCain. They had a 17-year-old kid last summer who had graduated from high school, who they assumed was going on to college. Then he went and signed up for the Marine Corps without their permission and without talking to them, which means he's going to Iraq. In fact, he's already been. He's home now, but he's going back. But the McCains didn't want to talk about that. They just do not want to talk about their son. I think part of it is that they don't want to put him in trouble over there, but they also don't want to wear it on their sleeves. I think there is something noble about that.

What's particularly important is that this is a family in which the father would say we have to increase the troops knowing full well that his son is going to be on the line. That's something a lot of Americans respect. We don't have many people like this. Most of the men and women who voted to send people to this war are sending somebody else's kids, not their own. General Ray Odierno, who's just taking over for Petraeus, is in the same situation. His son got his arm blown off over there, and Odierno's going back. Petraeus has a son in ROTC who may go before this is over.

So McCain has got all these likeable qualities but, his policies, I think, are open to question, especially in foreign policy. It's not just Iraq and wanting to win. There's a legitimate argument about how long we should stay. But if Iran gets to the point of having a nuclear weapon, if we're faced with a choice between letting them have the weapon and enacting a policy of deterrence versus taking them out militarily, he's going to take them out. And that is not a choice that many officers in the United States Army want to make. They are very, very anxious not to get into a military conflict in Iran. They do not want a bombing campaign, because they do not think it will work, and they fear they will be dragged in over there.

So how do you get Iran to cooperate? Most serious analysts of the situation say if you've got to get Russia to help put pressure on Iran, that Russia is very, very important in this complex chess game. So what is McCain doing? McCain is picking a fight with the Russians. He gave a speech recently on the west coast saying that we should have a league of democracies, and that we ought to throw Russia out of the G8. And we ought to invite in Brazil and India, by the way, and leave out China. You can't do that. If John McCain as president throws Russia out of the G8, you can kiss off the possibility they're going to be helpful on Iran.

And there are issues on the domestic front as well. George Bush cut taxes a lot and look at the growth rates we got. McCain wants to double that—without regard to the massive deficits. And by the way, he's for capping trade. At least he's not in denial on carbon and global warming. But in the same breath that he's proposing capping trade, he says, "let's have a holiday on tax payments for gasoline," which is exactly the wrong policy if you wish to reduce the amount of gasoline being used.

I want to end where I began—on the challenges that lie ahead. They are immense. In the first year of the next presidency, one-half of the Oval Office desk is going to be stacked with all the messes and all the complications of the international scene—whether it's Iraq, Iran, or Pakistan. They will all be very, very difficult to deal with. On the other side of the desk will be the repercussions from the current economic squeeze. And we don't yet know how big those repercussions will be. We do know they're going to bedevil the next president. The Bush administration was expecting deficits of $400 billion this year. After only six months we're at $313 billion. So the deficits are climbing, and that's going to have an enormous impact on the next president. That's Year One.

In Year Two, the Bush tax cuts expire and there could be a massive fight over revising the tax code. It always takes a lot of time to revise the tax code, but you have no choice. If you let the tax code expire, and you let all the taxes go back to where they were, you get the biggest tax increase since the Second World War. That's not going to happen. There's going to be a big fight to figure out where the adjustments will be made.

Year Three: the baby boomers start to retire en masse, the wave hits the shore, and our entitlement programs are all going to be under enormous pressure. We've not yet been able to revise our retirement program, and the next president is going to be under enormous pressure to do what no other president has been able to achieve.

And then Year Four—the Kyoto agreement expires. And not only is that going to mean dealing with energy and carbon in the United States, but it also has enormous consequences on how well the president leads internationally, especially with China and India. That's going to be a huge, huge requirement, and perhaps along with nuclear proliferation, is in many ways the transcendent issue that faces the next president.

So that's a massive, massive set of responsibilities. And that's why I think it's going to be very tough. Will the candidates be up to it? Are they going to be up to it? I'm just not sure. But I don't think you should write off the United States. We're a very resilient country. We have an economist, Charlie Schultz of the Brookings Institution, who observed once that the U.S. is not very good when we have termites in the basement, but we're terrific when we have a wolf at the door. And there are a lot of wolves out there right now. And in that sense, I hope we will draw together after this very, very messy campaign. And if not, then we take refuge in Bismark's theory that God does look after fools, drunkards, and the United States of America. So we have hope. We always have hope.

Q: Can you address the issue of populism in the United States a little more fully?
A: It must be emphasized that there are as many advantages that come out of trade as there are disadvantages, and that Americans do not fully appreciate the advantages. In many, many cases, we see people screaming that they're getting hurt in this new world. They blame it on trade, even though it may not be because of trade. It may

be thanks to technology, it may be due to a lot of other factors.

Capitalism has a creative and destructive force about it. We know that. But nonetheless there are a growing number of people who now see NAFTA as a symbol of what's gone wrong and what's hurting them in their lives. And when people voted in Ohio in the Democratic primary, 80 percent said trade was bad for Ohio. In Canada, I'm sure the numbers would be quite the reverse. We've always had a protectionist streak in the United States. Senator Packwood used to say that in any given year at any given time, at least one-third of the Senate would vote protectionist. And the question always becomes how much higher does that go? We're in a situation now where that figure is going up, not down. And it's going to require a certain amount of firm leadership and education on the benefits of trade.

John McCain has addressed it, but he's much more concerned about foreign policy. I've heard he has a tendency to get a little impatient with domestic issues, so I don't see him making a big issue of this. On the Democratic side there's been pure panic, and both candidates are getting themselves boxed in.

When Bilsby sat down with the Canadians and then the memo was leaked, that was very damaging. It forced Obama to be much more precise about where he stood. And Clinton has never been a great advocate of NAFTA. Does that mean they're going to wreck NAFTA? I don't think so. Does that mean that they want to reopen some sections? I think it's possible. Bill Clinton, I'm told, was here in Canada a couple of weeks ago and said don't worry about this in Canada, it's really about Mexico. And I think there's some truth to that, that most of the attention and concern has been about Mexico. But even so, if you go back and renegotiate with the Mexicans, you have to believe that Canadians will be drawn into it as well. So we need to take these trade arguments seriously because these candidates are starting to make commitments on the campaign trail that are going to be darn hard to break once they get in.

There is a lot of serious talk about taking a pause on trade negotiations, which is a mistake. We know from long history that once you stop going forward on a bicycle, you can fall off. It would be far, far better to keep going. I think it would be a very, very helpful thing to advise all of the presidential candidates, the two or maybe even three if this goes on, to visit Canada, to have some serious discussions, wide-ranging discussion, about a variety of economic issues. And so, you're not calling Barack up here to say we're going to put pressure on you on NAFTA. That would be a terrible mistake. He's not going to do that. But on the other hand, I think it would be very helpful for him to understand the perspectives of people not in his campaign, and not just out on the trail. Because there are different perspectives, and he is not a person who historically is so rigid that he can't change. On capital gains, for example, he's been out on the campaign trail saying he's going to raise capital gains rate in the United States to maybe 30 percent. And then some people got to him and he realized it was too high, and he said well maybe 20 percent. There needs to be a quiet migration away from these more rigid positions to put this back into a better place and to understand just how vital the trade questions are for the world.

I have friends on the Republican side who are big free traders who have been the negotiators in the past, who are worried that we're into a 1930s-type mentality on these questions of protectionism. I think that's extreme. The NAFTA agreement would not have passed this Congress, and it will certainly not pass the next Congress. I happened to be there in the Clinton administration. The White House was a big believer in NAFTA and worked hard on trying to get it passed. And it was still a hard struggle to get it. But we may have oversold it. I look back upon those days and worry that we oversold the benefits in order to get the votes. But we were down, and we thought it was very important for North America.

Q: Usually, in the first session of Congress, there's a very major policy that is being debated—like the Reagan tax cuts, for example. What will be the new policy? Is it possible we'll have a president saying let's retreat from the world?

A: I think the trade issue is an exception that sort of stands out. It's glaring, because it's such a departure from where we've been in the past. But if you look at the candidates, I actually think with any one of the three we will have more engagement with the world than we've had in recent years. I think we'll have less unilateralism, less of the arrogance of the early Bush years. I think you're going to find far more engagement with the world, and far more of an effort to seek solutions.

There is a deep-seated uneasiness in the American public that we're not playing a responsible role. People are very, very disturbed by the loss of reputation we've experienced. Americans find it humiliating to go overseas and be treated with disdain. So you can't underestimate this. We would also like to have a dollar we can actually go overseas with. That would help us some. In that sense, I think we are going to have more engagement and more talking by whoever gets elected. And it is possible that on Iran, for example, that just the process of talking—and taking off the table that we're going to obliterate them—might help, regardless of what happens on the nuclear side. The problem all along has been that Bush won't talk to them. And he's left the impression that whatever else happens, he'd still like to get rid of them.

I think you're going to find that type of attitude going off the table and that people are going to be in a somewhat different posture on a diplomatic offensive. So I'm less worried about that than I am worried about whether the United States is going to enter a period in which economic strength moves to the east. And in many ways probably the greatest story of our time is going to be that—not Iraq, Iran and all the rest. And the United States has not fully adjusted to this idea. But my biggest concern has been whether we're going to have the kind of leadership that would ensure the continuing strength of America and continuing multilateral leadership in the years ahead. I'm seriously of the view that unless we change the way we do business, unless we address some of these domestic issues as well as foreign policy issues, that there's a real chance that we will go into decline.

Back in the 1980s, Paul Kennedy wrote books about declinism. I think they were premature, but I think there are now signs that it's more serious than it was before. I believe that the United States is now in a strategic inflection point—to borrow a phrase from Andy Rove—and that a great deal depends on what kind of decisions we make. Are we capable of governing ourselves in a responsible way? Are we capable of taking on serious issues at home while also working with others to deal with large international questions? And I'm not sure I know the answer to that question right now, but I think it's a question that hangs over us as a people.

When I look at the day-to-day scuffling in Washington and the dysfunctionality of Washington, I can get very discouraged. But when I look at the history of the country—when it's really pressed and when there's good strong leadership, extraordinary leadership such as Franklin Roosevelt's—then I can take heart, and feel we can still pull this out. I don't know which way we're going to go on that, but I don't think you can count America out. It's a very resilient country when we finally understand and face up to the realities.

Here's my favorite story about leadership. It's about Franklin Roosevelt as the Second World War approached. Roosevelt, with George Marshall at his side, came to understand that we were going to be called upon to send far more than men and women in combat to the European theatre—that it was imperative that we also provide planes, guns, tanks, munitions. He came to understand that we had to become the arsenal of democracy, and that we would have to do that as well in the Pacific theater. And so Roosevelt went to his advisers and said, "how many planes are we building a year in the United States?" And they said "Mr. President, about six or seven thousand." And he said, "Okay, how many could we build if we tried harder?" They said probably 25,000. And he said, "That sounds great, but it's not sufficient." And so he went out against their advice, over their objections, and proclaimed that the goal of the United States would be to produce 50,000 planes a year. And everybody scoffed at that. Experts said it couldn't be done. And Roosevelt said, "You don't understand what this nation can do when we pull together." And he called in a lot of CEOs and had them convert their manufacturing plants into munitions plants, especially in the Detroit area, and he ran around the country and rallied people. And by the end of the war we were not producing 50,000 planes a year. The United States at the end of the war was producing 75,000 planes a year.

That's how Americans think of themselves, would like to think of themselves, as still being. The question is, can our leadership help to reawaken that kind of spirit and pull people together and let us get beyond the divisive politics we've found ourselves with for so long? And that's why I hope this election does bring change. It's so clearly necessary for the future of our country, and in many ways, for the future of the world.

ABOUT THE CONTRIBUTORS

Camille Paglia: Acknowledged as a leading social critic and educator, she came to prominence in 1990 after publishing the highly acclaimed book *Sexual Personae*. Her other works include *Sex, Art, and American Culture* and the 1994 collection *Vamps and Tramps*, which dealt with such celebrities as Bill and Hillary Clinton. Her latest book on poetry, *Break, Blow, Burn*, has also met with critical and commercial success. She is currently a professor at the University of the Arts in Philadelphia and writes a political column for Salon.com.

Shelby Steele is a leading expert in the study of race relations in the United States. In 2006, he received the Bradley Prize for his work. In 1991, his documentary work *Seven Days in Bensonhurst* won an Emmy. Dr. Steele received the National Book Critic's Circle Award for his book *The Content of Our Character*. He has also written *A Dream Deferred: The Second Betrayal of Black Freedom in America*.

His most recent book is *A Bound Man: Why We Are Excited about Obama and Why He Can't Win*. He is currently a senior fellow at the Hoover Institution at Stanford and writes regularly for *The New York Times* and *Wall Street Journal*.

James Carville: A controversial and colorful personality, Carville is one of America's most recognized political consultants and media pundits. He also runs a successful international political consulting business. Also known as the "Ragin' Cajun," Carville gained national attention for his work as the lead strategist of the successful 1992 presidential campaign of then–Arkansas Governor Bill Clinton. Carville was the co-host of CNN's *Crossfire* and appears regularly on its political show *The Situation Room*. His latest book is *Take It Back: A Battle Plan for Democratic Victory*.

David Gergen has been a well-known and respected commentator, author and adviser to presidents for thirty years. He served as director of communications for President Reagan and held positions in the administrations of Presidents Nixon, Ford and Clinton. He currently teaches at the John F. Kennedy School of Government at Harvard University and is editor-at-large at *U.S. News & World Report*. In the fall of 2000 he published the best-selling *Eyewitness to Power: The Essence of Leadership, Nixon to Clinton*. Gergen is also a political commentator for CNN.

ABOUT THE EDITORS

Patrick Luciani is co-director of the Salon Speakers Series. His background is in economics and public policy. He is currently a member of Massey College at the University of Toronto and senior fellow at the Atlantic Institute for Market Studies. He is a graduate of the John F. Kennedy School of Government at Harvard.

Rudyard Griffiths is co-director of the Salon Speakers Series. Rudyard is also the co-founder of the Canadian think tank The Dominion Institute and is an adviser to the Woodrow Wilson Center in Washington, D.C. Rudyard writes a regular column on Canadian issues and international affairs for the *National Post*. He has edited various books on Canadian history and politics. Rudyard serves on the boards of the Stratford Festival and Adrienne Clarkson's Canadian Institute for Citizenship. In 2006, he was recognized as one of Canada's Top 40 under 40. He is a graduate of Emmanuel College, Cambridge.